SURVIVING TEENAGE CHAOS

a hilarious guide to navigating high school missteps, friendship fumbles, and embarrassing moments

by ChatGPT and
Paul Lloyd Hemphill

Also by Paul Lloyd Hemphill
(with serious vibes)

BOOKS
Gettysburg Lessons In The Digital Age
Why You're Already A Leader
Inspiration For Teens
Inspiration For Skeptics
Max Your Leadership*!*
You're Awesome!
Planning For College
How To Play The College Game
and
(not so serious vibes)
Funnies of the Presidents (ChatGPT)
Watching Paint Dry (ChatGPT)

VIDEOS
America's 52 Stories

To teenagers facing school challenges.
Embrace your chaos with a smile, and
never underestimate the power of a good
laugh to get you through high school!

This non-fiction book is available for educational, business, or promotional use. Who knew learning could be this fun? For more information, contact the author directly at paul@inspirationforteens.com

Surviving Teenage Chaos

1. Young Adult Fiction 2. Teen Humor 3. High School Fiction
4. Coming-Of-Age 5. Contemporary fiction

TABLE OF CONTENTS

INTRODUCTION

Welcome to high school, where every day feels like a new adventure —or a chaotic comedy show!

Between navigating hallways, surviving pop quizzes, and figuring out where to sit at lunch, high school is full of awkward, funny, and unforgettable moments.

This fun book is your guide to laughing through it all.

Expect to see relatable stories about cafeteria drama, embarrassing missteps, and the weird quirks of teachers and classmates.

You'll learn that everyone feels awkward sometimes, and the best way to survive it all is with a good sense of humor. So buckle up, laugh often, and enjoy the ride!

ChatGPT and Paul Lloyd Hemphill

Chapter 1: The Locker Room of Doom

Let's get one thing straight—no matter how bad your day at high school is going, nothing can prepare you for the sheer terror that awaits in the gym locker room. Forget about the quizzes you bombed, the lunch trays you dropped in front of your crush, or even the fact that you accidentally called your math teacher "Mom" in front of the entire class. All of that fades into insignificance when you're faced with the ultimate teenage nightmare: changing in front of your peers.

With all the advancements of modern society, you'd think we would have figured out a way to make changing for gym class less traumatic. But here we are, still stuck in cramped locker rooms, surrounded by endless rows of metal lockers, flickering fluorescent lights, and the unmistakable scent of old gym socks. There's nothing quite like the experience of standing there, awkwardly trying to change clothes while pretending no one else can see you. Spoiler alert: everyone can.

The worst part of the locker room experience isn't even the changing itself—though that's its own kind of nightmare. It's the knowledge that every move you make is being witnessed by at least five other people, each of whom is mentally filing away your most embarrassing moments to discuss at lunch later. You know the drill: you're trying to change as quickly as humanly possible, but somehow, your shirt gets stuck over your head, or you drop your pants just as someone walks by. And let's not forget the ultimate wardrobe malfunction—mismatched socks. Nothing screams, "I have my life together" like two socks that don't belong in the same drawer, let alone on the same pair of feet.

But let's not forget the true stars of the locker room: the *showers*. These things are straight out of a horror movie. Sure, they're there for a reason, but has anyone ever actually used them? I'm convinced they're haunted. Every time you glance at them, they're dripping water, even though no one has touched them in years. It's as if they're crying for help—probably from all the germs festering inside them. I wouldn't go near one without a hazmat suit, and even then, I'd think twice.

And don't even get me started on the anxiety of *forgetting* your gym clothes. It's the perfect storm of teenage horror. You've got two choices: either face the wrath of your gym teacher and risk detention for not dressing out, or—worse—borrow someone else's spare clothes. Spoiler alert: those clothes are never your size. They're either too big, too small, or just plain itchy. Wearing them guarantees a day's worth of ridicule. It's like trying to run a marathon in a clown costume—uncomfortable, embarrassing, and impossible to forget.

The Fitness Test: Torture Disguised as Physical Education

As if the locker room experience isn't enough, let's talk about the fitness test. This isn't just a test of your physical endurance; it's a test of your mental fortitude and your ability to fake an injury at the perfect moment. The mile run, the sit-ups, the push-ups... it's a checklist designed to make you question every life decision that led you to this point. And let's not forget the dreaded *pacer test*—a beeping, soul-crushing gauntlet of misery.

Let's start with the mile run. Four laps around the track. Sounds simple enough, right? Wrong. Running a mile in gym class isn't about fitness—it's about survival. You're not just trying to complete the run; you're trying not to die of embarrassment in front of your classmates. There's always that one kid who sprints ahead like they're training for the Olympics, making the rest of us feel like we're wading through quicksand. You know the type—the one who finishes the mile in under six minutes without breaking a sweat, while the rest of us are gasping for breath halfway through the first lap. It's not just a run—it's a battle for dignity.

But the mile run isn't just about finishing. No, no, no. It's about timing. Your gym teacher is standing at the finish line with a stopwatch, calling out times as students cross the line. Everyone is watching as you stumble through the last few meters, legs wobbling, chest heaving, praying that you don't collapse before you reach the end. And when your time is finally announced? Let's just say it's not going to be your proudest moment.

Then there's the pacer test, designed to push you to the brink of physical and emotional exhaustion. You start out feeling confident, running back and forth between the lines as the beeps keep time. But as the intervals get shorter and the beeps get faster, that confidence quickly gives way to despair. You start to wonder if this is how it all ends—in a sweaty gym, face down on the floor, while your classmates jog past you. The worst part? The test doesn't stop when you're tired. It stops when you fail—publicly, painfully, and with no hope of redemption.

Awkward Sports Moments: A Study in Humiliation

Now, let's move on to the actual sports part of gym class. As much as we like to pretend it doesn't matter, it does. Whether it's dodgeball, volleyball, or basketball, one thing is guaranteed: there will be awkward moments, and they will haunt you for the rest of your high school career. Whether it's trying to catch a ball and watching it bounce off your face, or attempting to hit a volleyball only to miss entirely, gym class has a way of making you feel like you've never seen a ball in your life.

Take dodgeball, for example. It's notorious for creating moments of pure humiliation. If you've ever been the last person standing on your team, you know exactly what I'm talking about. The pressure is on. All eyes are on you. You're standing there, frozen, as the other team lines up their throws like they're preparing for the Hunger Games. And then, before you can even blink, you're hit square in the stomach, and it's all over. Game, dignity, and social status—gone in the blink of an eye.

And then there's the issue of trying to impress your crush during gym class. Spoiler alert: it never ends well. In theory, it seems like the perfect opportunity to show off your athletic prowess. But in reality, it's a recipe for disaster. You think you're going to look cool, but instead, you end up tripping over your own feet, missing every shot, and possibly injuring yourself in the process. There's nothing quite like trying to look smooth while dodging a flying ball to remind you that gym class is *not* the place for romance.

Gym Class Showers: The Stuff of Nightmares

Of all the horrors gym class has to offer, the showers are perhaps the most universally feared. No one uses them—no one *wants* to use them—but they're there, lurking in the background like a bad dream you can't escape. The very thought of showering at school, in front of your classmates, is enough to send shivers down your spine. It's like being asked to perform a magic trick while blindfolded—there's just no way it's going to end well.

The showers themselves are another story. They're always wet, even though no one has used them in years. It's as if they have a life of their own, dripping ominously in the background like some kind of creepy locker room ghost. The floor is perpetually slippery, and the drains are always clogged with unidentifiable substances. You'd rather take your chances with the pacer test than step foot in one of those showers.

But there's always that one brave soul who dares to use the showers, whether out of necessity or sheer madness. You watch them from a safe distance, equal parts fascinated and horrified, as they navigate the slippery tiles and attempt to rinse off under the weakest water pressure imaginable. They emerge not victorious, but changed. They've stared into the abyss, and the abyss has stared back. Honestly, you're not sure they'll ever be the same.

Final Thoughts: How to Survive the Locker Room of Doom

If there's one thing high school gym class teaches you, it's that survival is less about fitness and more about learning to laugh at yourself. The locker room may be terrifying, the fitness test may be torture, and the sports may be humiliating, but at the end of the day, it's all part of the high school experience.

So, how do you survive? You embrace the chaos. Forget about impressing anyone, and focus on getting through it with your sense of humor intact. Laugh at the awkward moments, make peace with the fact that you'll never master dodgeball, and always, always "forget" your gym clothes on test day. Because when it comes to the locker room of doom, the real victory is in making it out alive—and with a story to tell.

Chapter 2: Drama Class — And We're Not Talking About Theater

If there's one universal truth about high school, it's this: the drama is inevitable. No, I'm not talking about the theater department, where actual acting takes place. I'm talking about the kind of drama that seems to thrive in the hallways, lunchrooms, and group chats of high school students everywhere. It's the drama that bubbles up out of nowhere, spreads faster than Wi-Fi, and often leaves everyone involved wondering how things escalated so quickly.

At first glance, high school drama may seem harmless—just a few hurt feelings, a little gossip here and there—but in reality, it's a force to be reckoned with. A simple misunderstanding can turn into an all-out battle, and once rumors start flying, there's no stopping them. High school drama is like a soap opera that never ends, except no one has a script, and the plot twists are even more ridiculous. The best part? Everyone is starring in it, whether they want to or not.

Rumors: The Social Media of the Hallways

Rumors are the backbone of high school drama. They start small, usually with something as innocent as "Did you hear what so-and-so said?" And before you know it, the entire school is buzzing with new information—information that is almost always exaggerated or completely untrue. A simple comment can turn into a full-blown conspiracy in the span of a single lunch period.

Let's break it down. Imagine this scenario: you're walking through the hallway, minding your own business, when you overhear someone say, "Did you hear that Emily is moving?" A totally innocent comment, right? But by the time that rumor makes its rounds, it has somehow evolved into, "Emily is moving to Alaska to join a reality show about ice fishing." The most ridiculous part? Half the school will believe it. People will start asking Emily about her upcoming ice-fishing career, and she'll be left wondering how a simple comment about visiting her aunt for the weekend turned into this.

Rumors are the high school equivalent of viral social media posts. Once they're out there, you can't take them back, and they spread at lightning speed. And just like with social media, the more outrageous the rumor, the faster it spreads. It doesn't matter how outlandish it sounds—if it's juicy, it's going to make the rounds. When in doubt, always remember this golden rule: *if you didn't hear it directly from the source, it's probably nonsense*.

The Art of Ignoring Drama

One of the best ways to survive high school drama is to master the art of ignoring it. I know, I know—easier said than done. When drama is swirling around you, it's hard not to get sucked in. But trust me, ignoring drama is a skill that will save you a lot of headaches.

The first step to becoming a drama-ignoring pro is learning when to keep your mouth shut. You don't have to have an opinion on every little thing that happens. In fact, the less you say, the better. When in doubt, pretend you didn't hear anything. If someone asks you, "Did you hear what happened with Sarah and Jake?" you can just shrug and say, "Nope!" This does two things: it keeps you out of the loop, and it sends a signal that you're not interested in participating in the drama.

Another key to avoiding drama is knowing when to walk away. Picture this: you're at your locker, and you overhear a group of people gossiping about a fight that happened in the cafeteria. You can feel the curiosity tugging at you, begging you to ask for details. But resist! If you stick around and start asking questions, you're officially involved. Walking away may seem difficult, but it's the best way to ensure you don't end up in the middle of someone else's conflict.

Let's not forget that some drama is unavoidable. If you find yourself caught in the crossfire of a particularly intense situation, your best bet is to stay as neutral as possible. Think of yourself as Switzerland—no sides, no opinions, just peace and neutrality. The less you involve yourself, the faster the drama will pass you by. In high school, people have a short attention span when it comes to drama. There will always be something new to talk about, and if you don't engage, they'll move on to the next big thing.

Frenemies: The Most Dangerous Kind of Friend

Of all the types of drama that exist in high school, *frenemy* drama is by far the most complicated. A frenemy is a unique combination of friend and enemy—someone you hang out with, but who also drives you completely insane. They're the person who will compliment your new shoes while subtly hinting that they don't match your outfit. Frenemies are experts at delivering backhanded compliments and creating drama without even trying. The worst part? You can never tell if they're being genuine or if they're secretly plotting your downfall.

Navigating frenemy relationships requires a delicate balance. On the one hand, you don't want to start a full-blown fight and escalate things. On the other hand, you don't want to let them walk all over you. The key is to maintain a sense of humor and not take anything too personally. Frenemies thrive on getting a reaction, so the less you react, the less power they have over you.

Here's a typical frenemy scenario: You walk into school feeling pretty good about your outfit. You've got on your favorite sweater, and you're feeling confident. Then your frenemy approaches you and says, "Oh my gosh, I love your sweater! I had one just like it... in middle school." Ouch. It's the kind of comment that sounds like a compliment but has just enough sting to make you second-guess your entire wardrobe. The trick here is not to let it get under your skin. Just smile and say, "Thanks! I guess classic styles never go out of fashion!" By turning the situation into a joke, you take away their power and come out on top.

Remember, frenemies are all about subtle competition. They want to one-up you without being obvious about it. The best way to handle this is by not playing their game. If they're bragging about their latest achievement, congratulate them, but don't feel the need to compete. Frenemies thrive on rivalry, and by opting out of the competition, you're denying them the satisfaction.

The Exaggerated Fight: How Did We Get Here?

High school fights are the stuff of legend. I'm not talking about physical fights—though those happen too—I'm talking about the verbal, dramatic, over-the-top kind of fights that seem to blow up out of nowhere. One minute you're chatting with your best friend about what to get for lunch, and the next minute, you're in a heated argument over who gets to sit in the front seat on the way home. How does it happen? No one really knows. But it happens all the time.

The thing about high school fights is that they're rarely about what they seem to be about. Sure, you're technically arguing about the front seat, but in reality, it's probably about something much deeper—like that time your friend didn't invite you to her sleepover, or the fact that she borrowed your favorite hoodie and never gave it back. High school fights are like icebergs: you only see the tip, but there's a whole lot more going on beneath the surface.

The worst part about these fights is that they tend to escalate quickly. What starts as a minor disagreement can quickly turn into an all-out war, with both sides dragging their friends into the fray for support. Before you know it, half the school is taking sides, and everyone is talking about who's "Team A" and who's "Team B." It's like a soap opera, except everyone is a main character, and the drama is somehow both ridiculous and deeply personal at the same time.

Here's a tip for handling high school fights: when things start getting heated, take a deep breath and ask yourself, "Is this really worth it?" Nine times out of ten, the answer will be no. Most fights can be avoided if one person is willing to take a step back and de-escalate the situation. It may not feel satisfying in the moment, but trust me, you'll thank yourself later when you're not spending your lunch period locked in a cold war with your best friend.

Tips for Surviving High School Drama

Surviving high school drama isn't easy, but it's not impossible either. With a little humor and a lot of patience, you can make it through with your sanity intact. Here are some quick tips to help you navigate the drama-filled waters of high school:

1. **Don't take everything personally**: High school is full of people trying to figure out who they are, and sometimes that means they'll say or do things that hurt your feelings. Try not to take it to heart—it's usually not about you.

2. **Know when to walk away**: If you see drama brewing, don't be afraid to remove yourself from the situation. You don't have to be involved in every conflict, and sometimes the best thing you can do is stay out of it.

3. **Keep things in perspective**: Remember that high school is just one chapter of your life. The things that feel like the end of the world right now will seem much less important in a few years.

4.   **Laugh it off**: When in doubt, laugh. High school drama can be ridiculous, but that's part of what makes it so entertaining. If you can find the humor in the situation, it'll be a lot easier to handle.

5.   **Stay true to yourself**: At the end of the day, the best way to survive high school drama is to be yourself. Don't change who you are to fit in with others, and don't let the drama get in the way of enjoying your high school experience.

Chapter 3: Friendship Fumbles

If there's one thing that defines the high school experience—aside from pop quizzes, gym class disasters, and the drama that spreads faster than Wi-Fi—it's friendship. Friends are the lifeblood of high school. They're the people who help you survive the chaos, laugh with you about inside jokes, and occasionally make you question your life choices. But let's face it, teen friendships are also full of *epic* fumbles. No one really teaches you how to be a perfect friend. You're all just winging it, figuring out how to navigate the ups and downs together—and the result? A lot of hilariously awkward moments.

In this chapter, we'll dive into the unpredictable world of teen friendships. From awkward first introductions to misinterpreted text messages, and from inside jokes that leave everyone else scratching their heads to the perils of ghosting, this is your guide to surviving—and laughing at—the inevitable fumbles of high school friendships.

Awkward First Introductions: "Hey, Didn't We…? Oh, Never Mind"

Let's start with the awkward beginnings of most high school friendships. Contrary to popular belief, not all friendships start with a magical moment where two people just "click." In fact, a lot of them begin with something painfully awkward—like the infamous "Hey, didn't we meet…? Oh wait, never mind" scenario.

Imagine this: It's your first day of high school. You're already on edge because, well, it's *high school* and you don't know anyone. You sit down in your homeroom class, nervously fidgeting with your backpack straps, when you spot a familiar face across the room. "Hey!" you call out, feeling confident. "Didn't we go to middle school together?"

The person looks at you, tilts their head, and says, "Uh... I don't think so?"

Cue the awkward silence. You've just embarrassed yourself in front of a potential new friend, and there's no way to backpedal without making things worse. The rest of the class period is spent avoiding eye contact and silently praying for the bell to ring.

This, my friends, is how a lot of high school friendships begin: with confusion, mistaken identity, and the type of awkwardness that makes you wish you could disappear into the floor. But sometimes, the awkwardness is exactly what breaks the ice, and after a few awkward conversations, you and your new friend are bonding over the shared misery of surviving your first week of school.

Misreading the Text Message: "Wait, Were You Being Serious?"

One of the most common—and hilarious—friendship fumbles of the teen years comes in the form of misinterpreted text messages. It's hard enough to understand sarcasm in real life, but add the mystery of texting into the mix, and things can go from "haha" to "uh oh" in no time.

Let's say you're texting your friend about a class assignment. You send a message that says, "Ugh, this project is the worst. I'm literally going to die." In your head, you're being totally sarcastic. But your friend reads it and panics. "OMG, are you okay?" they reply, completely missing the joke.

Now you're stuck trying to figure out how to explain that no, you're not in actual danger, and yes, you were just being dramatic. The text exchange devolves into a confusing mess of "lol's" and "jk's" as you both try to clear things up. By the end of it, your friend is convinced you're secretly hiding a crisis, and you're left wondering why anyone ever invented texting in the first place.

But it doesn't stop there. Misreading texts can happen in a variety of ways. Sometimes you send a joke, and your friend takes it seriously. Other times, your friend sends a message that seems totally normal, but you read way too much into it. Suddenly, a simple "K" feels like the beginning of the end of your friendship.

Here's a pro tip: When in doubt, assume your friend is joking. It's better to laugh it off than to spend hours decoding the meaning behind a text. And remember, the "K" text is *not* a death sentence for your friendship—it's just your friend being too lazy to type out "Okay."

Inside Jokes: The Key to a Confusing Friendship

One of the greatest perks of having a close friend is the treasure trove of inside jokes that only the two of you understand. These jokes become your secret language, something that bonds you in a way that makes you feel invincible—until, of course, you try to use them in front of other people.

Picture this: You and your best friend are sitting at lunch, reminiscing about the time you both accidentally spilled orange juice on your math teacher's desk. It's an inside joke now, and you can't stop laughing about it. Your other friends, sitting nearby, look at you like you've lost your mind. "What's so funny?" they ask, confused.

You try to explain. "Well, we were in math class, and... uh, never mind, you had to be there."

The thing about inside jokes is that they only work if you *were* there. To everyone else, they sound bizarre, nonsensical, and occasionally a little bit concerning. But to you and your friend, they're the glue that holds your friendship together.

And inside jokes don't just stay confined to your lunch table—they sneak into every part of your life. Before you know it, you and your friend are sending each other texts filled with random words and phrases that would make no sense to anyone else. "Hey, remember 'pineapple pizza moment'?" you text, and your friend immediately replies with a string of laughing emojis, knowing exactly what you're talking about.

Inside jokes may confuse the heck out of everyone else, but they're a vital part of teen friendships. They're the moments that remind you of all the fun (and slightly weird) experiences you've shared. And let's be honest, making other people scratch their heads while you and your friend crack up is half the fun.

Accidentally Ghosting Your Friend: The Unintentional Fade-Out

In the world of teen friendships, ghosting is usually a big no-no. But what happens when you *accidentally* ghost someone? It's more common than you might think, and it often starts with something as simple as forgetting to reply to a text message.

Let's say your friend sends you a message: "Hey, wanna hang out this weekend?" You're in the middle of doing homework (or scrolling through social media), so you think, "I'll reply in a minute." But then you get distracted. A few hours go by, and then a day, and before you know it, it's been three days since your friend's message, and you never replied.

Now you're in a dilemma. Do you reply and pretend nothing happened? Do you apologize for ghosting? Or do you let it go and hope your friend doesn't think you're avoiding them?

The truth is, accidental ghosting happens to the best of us. Life gets busy, messages get buried, and suddenly you've unintentionally disappeared from your friend's radar. The trick to handling it is simple: own up to it. Send a quick message like, "OMG, I'm so sorry! I totally spaced out on replying!" Nine times out of ten, your friend will laugh it off and everything will go back to normal.

But what if you're the one being ghosted? The first instinct might be to panic —"Did I do something wrong? Is my friend mad at me?" But before you spiral into anxiety, take a deep breath and remind yourself that it's probably nothing. Your friend might have forgotten to reply, or they could be busy with other things. When in doubt, send a lighthearted follow-up message like, "Hey, did you get lost in the wilderness or something?" More often than not, your friend will respond with an "Oops!" and you'll be back to chatting like usual.

Misreading Sarcasm: "Wait, You Were Joking?"

Sarcasm: the lifeblood of many teen friendships, but also the source of some of the funniest misunderstandings. When you know someone well, sarcasm is second nature. You can throw out a sarcastic comment, and your friend will instantly get it. But every once in a while, the sarcasm doesn't land quite right, and that's when things get awkward.

Picture this: You and your friend are joking around, and you say, "Yeah, because *you're* totally the most organized person I know." You expect your friend to laugh, but instead, they look at you with wide eyes and say, "Wait… do you actually think I'm disorganized?"

Cue the awkward backpedaling. "No, no, I was just kidding!" you explain, but the damage is done. Your friend now believes that you think they're a disorganized mess, and you're stuck trying to convince them that it was just sarcasm.

The thing about sarcasm is that it doesn't always translate well in every situation—especially over text. You send what you think is an obviously sarcastic message, but your friend takes it seriously. Suddenly, you're in a full-blown misunderstanding that neither of you saw coming.

When it comes to sarcasm, the golden rule is to be mindful of how your friend might interpret it. If they're in a bad mood or feeling insecure about something, it might be best to tone down the sarcasm and stick to straightforward jokes. And if they misinterpret your sarcasm, don't panic— just laugh it off and move on

Chapter 4: Crush Catastrophes…The Awkwardness of Having a High School Crush

If there's one experience that defines the high school years, it's having a crush. A crush is like a tornado of emotions—exciting, nerve-wracking, and utterly embarrassing, all at the same time. It's that flutter in your stomach when your crush walks into the room, the sudden inability to form coherent sentences when they talk to you, and the overthinking that accompanies every interaction. Let's be real: having a high school crush is equal parts thrilling and mortifying.

In this chapter, we're going to explore all the awkwardness that comes with liking someone in high school. From accidentally sending texts to the wrong person to turning beet red every time your crush is nearby, these stories will remind you that everyone has experienced the cringe-worthy moments that come with navigating teenage romance. And remember, if you're going through this right now, here's some key advice: *Don't overthink it. No, really —stop overthinking it!*

The Wrong Words at the Wrong Time

One of the classic symptoms of having a high school crush is the sudden inability to speak like a normal human being. You might be a totally articulate person most of the time, but as soon as your crush shows up, your brain goes on vacation, and your mouth starts saying things you didn't even know were possible.

Picture this: You're sitting in class, trying to focus on the teacher's lecture about the Pythagorean theorem. You've got your notebook open, you're ready to take notes, and everything is going fine. Then it happens—your crush walks into the room. Suddenly, the Pythagorean theorem is the last thing on your mind. Your palms start to sweat, your heart beats faster, and you start frantically rehearsing what you're going to say if they talk to you.

But instead of playing it cool, you completely fumble the moment. Let's say your crush walks up to you and asks, "Hey, can I borrow a pencil?" This is your moment. You've got the perfect opportunity to have a normal conversation with them. But instead of replying with a simple "Sure," your brain short-circuits, and you blurt out, "Yeah, um, you can have all my pencils forever."

What? All your pencils *forever*? Why did you say that? You have no idea. You meant to say something casual, but now your crush is looking at you like you've just offered them your life savings. The conversation ends awkwardly, and you spend the rest of the day mentally replaying the interaction, cringing at every second.

Here's the thing about high school crushes: you will say the wrong thing at the wrong time. It's inevitable. But the good news is that it's never as bad as you think it is. Your crush probably doesn't even remember the awkward conversation, and if they do, they'll likely just find it endearing. So don't beat yourself up—chalk it up to the wonderful world of teen romance.

The Dreaded Wrong Text

In today's world, most of our interactions happen over text. While this is great for introverts who would rather not talk face-to-face, it also opens up a whole new realm of awkwardness—*especially* when it comes to texting your crush. There's nothing more terrifying than realizing you've sent the wrong message to the wrong person.

Imagine this scenario: You're texting your best friend about your crush. You're typing out a message like, "OMG, I can't stop thinking about them. They're so cute, and I'm dying every time they walk by." You hit send, and then it happens. You realize, with a sinking feeling in your stomach, that you didn't send the message to your best friend—you sent it to *your crush*.

Panic sets in. What do you do? Do you try to play it off as a joke? Do you pretend it never happened and hope they ignore it? Or do you just throw your phone into the nearest body of water and run away?

In moments like this, the key is to stay calm (easier said than done, I know). Depending on how well you know your crush, you can either laugh it off with a "Well, that was awkward, wasn't it?" or you can own the moment and say, "Oops, that wasn't meant for you, but it's true!" Either way, once the initial embarrassment fades, you'll realize that it wasn't the end of the world. In fact, it might even lead to a funny story you can tell your friends later.

The moral of the story? Double-check your texts before you hit send. And if you do send the wrong message, remember—it's not the end of the world. Your crush has probably done something just as embarrassing at some point.

Blushing: The Involuntary Betrayal

If there's one thing that every high schooler dreads when their crush is around, it's blushing. You might be trying your hardest to play it cool, but your body has other plans. The minute your crush walks by or looks in your direction, your face turns as red as a tomato, and there's nothing you can do to stop it.

Blushing is like a giant neon sign that says, "HEY, I LIKE YOU!" and it feels like everyone can see it. The more you try to stop blushing, the worse it gets. Your cheeks get hotter, your face gets redder, and you start to wonder if you'll ever be able to interact with your crush without looking like you've just run a marathon.

Take this example: You're sitting in the cafeteria with your friends, trying to act normal, when your crush walks by. You can feel them getting closer, and you try to act casual—maybe by pretending to laugh at something your friend said or staring intensely at your lunch tray like it's the most fascinating thing in the world. But then your crush stops at your table and says, "Hey, how's it going?"

Cue the blushing. Your face turns bright red, and suddenly, you can't make eye contact. You mumble something incoherent and hope your friends will jump in to save you. But nope, they're too busy watching the whole thing unfold like it's the most entertaining show they've ever seen.

Blushing is annoying, but here's the thing: it's completely normal. In fact, most people find blushing cute, not embarrassing. It shows that you're genuinely interested in someone, and it's nothing to be ashamed of. So the next time your face turns red around your crush, just own it. Smile, keep the conversation going, and know that your blush isn't betraying you—it's just a sign that you care.

Overthinking Every Interaction

If there's one thing that defines the experience of having a crush, it's overthinking. You overanalyze every single interaction with your crush, replaying it in your head on a loop like you're trying to solve a mystery. Did they smile at you on purpose, or were they just being polite? What did they mean when they said, "See you later"? Was that a hint that they want to hang out, or were they just saying goodbye?

Overthinking can turn the simplest interactions into complex puzzles. Let's say your crush texts you something like, "Hey, what's up?" On the surface, this is a totally normal message. But in your head, it becomes something much bigger. You start wondering why they texted you. Did they text you because they like you, or are they just being friendly? And what should you reply? Should you play it cool with a simple "Not much, you?" or should you try to be funny and impress them with a witty response? Suddenly, what should have been a quick reply has turned into a 20-minute mental debate.

Overthinking can also happen in person. You'll have a short conversation with your crush, and afterward, you'll spend hours analyzing every detail. "Did they laugh at my joke because it was funny, or were they just being polite?" "Did they stand closer to me than usual, or am I imagining it?" "Did they say 'see you later' because they *want* to see me later, or was it just a casual phrase?"

Here's the best advice you'll ever get when it comes to crushes: *Don't overthink it*. No, really—*stop overthinking it*. Most of the time, your crush is just as clueless and nervous as you are. They're probably not analyzing every word and gesture like you are, and they're definitely not expecting you to be perfect. So relax, go with the flow, and enjoy the fun (and awkwardness) of having a crush. Life is too short to spend it obsessing over every detail.

The Accidental Stare

Let's be honest: we've all been caught staring at our crush at least once. It's not something we plan—it just happens. You're sitting in class or walking down the hallway, and suddenly, you find yourself gazing at your crush, daydreaming about what it would be like if they liked you back. It's a harmless moment, right? Until they catch you staring.

The worst part about being caught staring is that there's no good way to recover from it. Once your crush makes eye contact, you have about 0.5 seconds to react, and most of the time, you panic. You either look away so quickly that it's obvious you were staring, or you awkwardly smile and try to pretend you were just casually looking around.

The truth is, everyone stares at their crush from time to time. It's part of the whole "having a crush" thing. So if you get caught staring, don't worry too much about it. Play it off with a smile, or just go about your business. Chances are, your crush has been caught staring at someone before, too.

Final Thoughts: Embrace the Awkwardness

Having a crush in high school is a rollercoaster of emotions. One minute you're on cloud nine because your crush smiled at you, and the next minute you're cringing because you said something awkward. But that's all part of the experience. The awkward moments, the blushing, the overthinking—they're what make having a crush so memorable.

So embrace the awkwardness. Don't be afraid to laugh at yourself when things don't go as planned. At the end of the day, everyone has gone through the same thing, and the embarrassing moments are the ones that you'll look back on and laugh about later. And who knows? Maybe one day, your crush will remember the time you gave them all your pencils forever, and they'll laugh about it, too.

Chapter 5: Fashion Faux Pas

High school is a time of great change, both internally and externally. While the internal changes often involve discovering who you are and what you stand for, the external ones can feel just as critical. One of the most intense areas of this transformation? Fashion. The desire to keep up with ever-changing trends, the occasional (or frequent) wardrobe malfunction, and the seemingly impossible task of looking good on school picture day all make for a chaotic, and often hilarious, adventure in personal style.

In this chapter, we'll dive into the many fashion faux pas that define the high school experience. From bad hair days that refuse to be tamed to questionable outfits that seemed like a good idea at the time, we'll explore how high school is often a parade of awkward and unforgettable fashion moments. And if you're currently in the midst of trying to find your style, here's one thing you should remember: *You're not alone.*

The Trend Game: Trying to Keep Up

One of the most challenging parts of high school fashion is trying to keep up with the latest trends. Trends come and go so fast that by the time you've convinced your parents to buy you that new pair of shoes everyone has, they're already out of style. Fashion in high school isn't just about looking good—it's about *fitting in*. And to fit in, you've got to know what's "in" right now, which is a full-time job.

Take, for example, the brief but intense reign of neon colors. One day, everyone was wearing muted earth tones, and the next, the hallways were awash in neon pink, green, and yellow. Suddenly, it seemed like if you weren't glowing in the dark, you were completely out of touch. So, you begged your parents to take you shopping, insisting that neon was *the* look. You even managed to get a neon green jacket, which you thought would make you look trendy and cool.

But the day you finally wore your new jacket to school, something felt off. Everyone else had already moved on to the next big thing—tie-dye, perhaps—and you were stuck glowing like a human highlighter. The worst part? No one told you that wearing neon wasn't just a trend; it was a temporary trend. So there you were, strutting through the hallways, turning heads—not because you looked amazing, but because you looked like a traffic cone.

And it's not just clothes. Hair trends, accessories, even the way you wear your backpack—all of it is subject to change at the drop of a hat. Remember the brief but powerful phase when people wore their backpacks with only one strap? It was all about looking effortlessly cool, even though using both straps was clearly more practical. But the pressure to follow the trend was strong, and everyone was walking around with lopsided backpacks, constantly adjusting their single strap so it didn't slide off their shoulders.

The lesson here? Fashion trends come and go, often leaving us looking back and wondering, "What was I thinking?" But at the time, it feels like life or death. Spoiler alert: it's not.

Bad Hair Days: When the Universe Conspires Against You

If there's one thing that's even more unpredictable than high school fashion trends, it's your hair. Your hair has a mind of its own, and it chooses the worst possible moments to rebel. There's nothing quite as soul-crushing as waking up on the day of a big event—like a school dance, or worse, picture day—only to find that your hair has decided to defy gravity in ways science can't explain.

Bad hair days are universal, but they feel *personal*. You could have the most carefully laid-out plan for your morning routine: wake up, shower, use your favorite styling product, and then blow-dry your hair into perfection. But somewhere between the shower and the mirror, everything goes wrong. Instead of sleek and shiny locks, you end up with frizz, cowlicks, and volume in all the wrong places. Suddenly, you're left staring at yourself, wondering if there's any way to salvage this disaster.

And let's not forget about bangs. At some point, we all thought bangs were a good idea. Maybe you saw someone on TV or in a magazine and thought, "I could pull that off." So, you asked your hairdresser (or worse, you did it yourself) for bangs, imagining that they would transform you into a chic, sophisticated version of yourself. What you didn't account for was the fact that bangs have *moods*. One day, they might lay perfectly across your forehead, framing your face like a celebrity's. The next day? They're sticking out in random directions, impossible to control, and making you regret every decision you've ever made.

The worst part of a bad hair day is that it's like a spotlight shining on your insecurities. You walk into school, and it feels like everyone is staring at your wild mane, when in reality, no one is paying as much attention as you think. Still, it's hard not to feel like your hair is a public spectacle.

But here's the truth: *Everyone* has bad hair days. It's a rite of passage. And while it may feel like the end of the world in the moment, you'll eventually laugh about the time your hair decided to channel its inner mad scientist on picture day.

The School Picture Disaster: Immortalizing the Embarrassment

Ah, school picture day—the day when you're supposed to look your best, but somehow always manage to look your worst. There's something about the combination of bad lighting, forced smiles, and the pressure to get everything perfect that guarantees a disaster.

You wake up early, determined to make this year's picture the one you won't cringe at every time you see it. You spend extra time on your hair, pick out your best outfit, and practice your smile in the mirror. You're ready. But the moment you sit down in front of that giant backdrop, it all falls apart.

First, the photographer tells you to tilt your head in a way that feels completely unnatural. Then they say, "Smile!" and what comes out is more of a grimace than a grin. Your eyes are half-closed, your hair has somehow flattened in the ten seconds it took you to walk to the camera, and your shirt collar is doing something weird that you didn't notice until it was too late.

The worst part? School pictures are forever. They get printed, handed out to relatives, and plastered in yearbooks for all eternity. And no matter how many times you promise yourself, "Next year will be better," the cycle repeats itself. It's like some kind of cosmic joke—no matter how hard you try, school picture day is destined to end in disappointment.

But here's the thing: Everyone's school pictures are a little awkward. Sure, there are always a few lucky people who somehow manage to look amazing in every single photo, but for the rest of us? School pictures are a snapshot of a time when we were still figuring things out. They're awkward, yes, but they're also a reminder that no one is perfect—and that's okay.

Dressing to Impress (and Failing Miserably)

One of the most common high school experiences is trying to dress to impress, only to end up looking ridiculous. Whether it's for a school dance, a big presentation, or just a regular day when you want to catch the attention of your crush, we've all tried to step up our fashion game—and failed spectacularly.

It usually starts with a vision. You've seen an outfit in a magazine or online that looks effortlessly cool, and you're determined to recreate it. You spend hours putting together the perfect combination of clothes, shoes, and accessories. You stand in front of the mirror, convincing yourself that you've nailed it.

But the moment you step outside, doubts start creeping in. Is this shirt too tight? Are these shoes too loud? Does this hat make me look like I'm trying too hard? By the time you get to school, you're overanalyzing every detail of your outfit, and what started as an attempt to look confident has turned into a full-blown fashion crisis.

And then it happens: someone makes an offhand comment that wasn't even meant to be negative, but it shatters your fragile confidence. "Cool shoes," they say. But all you hear is, "Those shoes are way too much for a Wednesday." Suddenly, you feel like you've made a huge mistake, and you spend the rest of the day hiding behind your locker, trying to blend in with the crowd.

The truth is, everyone has days when their fashion choices don't quite hit the mark. But here's the thing: fashion is all about trial and error. You're not going to get it right every time, and that's okay. What matters is that you're experimenting, trying new things, and figuring out what works for you. Sure, you might look back and cringe at some of your high school outfits, but those moments are what help you develop your personal style.

Final Thoughts: Embrace the Fashion Fumbles

High school fashion is a minefield of trends, bad hair days, and wardrobe disasters. But it's also a time to have fun with your style and not take yourself too seriously. The truth is, no one expects you to have it all figured out. The fashion faux pas, the awkward school pictures, and the bad hair days are all part of the process.

So embrace the fumbles. Wear the neon jacket, rock the bangs, and laugh at the time your hair rebelled on picture day. Because in the end, it's the mistakes and the awkward moments that make high school so memorable. And who knows? Maybe one day you'll look back at that traffic

Chapter 6: The Mystery of High School Hallways

Navigating the hallways of high school is nothing short of a heroic feat. Forget finding your place in the social hierarchy—just figuring out how to get from one classroom to another without a complete breakdown feels like an accomplishment. Whether you're a freshman just entering the labyrinth or a senior who's supposedly mastered it, the hallways of high school remain an enigma. They're chaotic, crowded, and riddled with obstacles that make a regular trip from homeroom to history class feel like an episode of *Survivor*.

In this chapter, we'll explore the many challenges of navigating high school hallways—from dodging stampedes of students to deciphering the complex, seemingly impossible layouts of school buildings. And yes, we'll also provide a humorous guide to hallway etiquette, because let's face it: some people need it.

Getting Lost: The First-Day Frenzy

Every high school student has experienced it: the panic that sets in when you realize you have no idea where your next class is. You thought you memorized the layout of the school during orientation, but now, as the bell rings and the crowd surges, you're utterly lost. It's like being dropped into the middle of a maze with no map and no way out.

Let's paint the picture: It's your first day of freshman year, and you've got your neatly printed schedule in hand. You've spent the last week preparing for this day, mentally mapping out the shortest routes to each of your classes. You even practiced your locker combination so you wouldn't be one of those kids holding up the line. But now, as you stand in the middle of the hallway, surrounded by what feels like a tidal wave of upperclassmen, none of that preparation matters. You're lost.

You take a deep breath, glance at your schedule, and start walking in what you *think* is the right direction. But five minutes later, you're pretty sure you've passed the same hallway three times, and you still haven't found

Room 204. The bell rings again—this time signaling that you're officially late—and your heart sinks as you consider the possibility of spending the next four years wandering the hallways like a lost soul in search of a classroom that may or may not exist.

Eventually, you give up and ask a passing student for directions, only to have them point to the door *right next to you*. Yep. You've been standing next to Room 204 this entire time. Cue the embarrassed laughter as you finally slip into class, hoping no one noticed how long it took you to find it.

The Hallway Stampede: Survival of the Fastest

Once you've figured out where your classes are, there's another challenge waiting for you: surviving the hallway stampede. Every high school has one—the mad rush between classes when the bell rings, and the hallways are suddenly filled with hundreds of students, all trying to get to their next class as quickly as possible. It's chaos. Pure, unfiltered chaos.

The key to surviving the stampede is speed and agility. You've got to be quick on your feet and ready to dodge at a moment's notice, or you'll get swept up in the crowd and carried to some unknown part of the school. Picture this: the bell rings, you've got five minutes to make it from your science class on the first floor to your math class on the third floor, and the hallways are jam-packed with people moving in every direction. You're not just walking—you're dodging, weaving, and occasionally sprinting, all while trying not to bump into anyone or drop your books.

One of the most dangerous parts of the stampede is the intersection—the spots where two or more hallways converge into a single, narrow space. These areas are like the highway on-ramp during rush hour: full of people trying to merge into a limited amount of space. If you're not careful, you'll end up trapped in a gridlock of backpacks and elbows, with no way out.

Then, there's the dreaded slow walker—the person who seems completely unaware that everyone around them is in a hurry. They're strolling along, taking their sweet time, completely oblivious to the fact that the hallway behind them is a mass of frustrated students trying to get by. The slow walker is the bane of every high school student's existence. You can either try to politely ask them to speed up (good luck with that), or you can attempt the risky maneuver of passing them in the narrow hallway, which usually results in an awkward dance of side-steps and apologies.

And let's not forget the occasional locker explosion. Just when you think you've got a clear path, someone's locker bursts open, sending textbooks, papers, and gym clothes flying into the hallway. It's like an obstacle course, except no one warned you that dodgeball would be part of the curriculum.

Hallway Etiquette: The Unspoken Rules

If there's one thing high school desperately needs, it's a handbook on hallway etiquette. There are so many unspoken rules that govern the flow of traffic in the hallways, and breaking any of them can result in glares, eye-rolls, and even an awkward confrontation with an upperclassman. So, let's break down the basics of hallway etiquette, shall we?

1. Don't Stop in the Middle of the Hallway
This rule cannot be emphasized enough. If you need to talk to your friend, check your phone, or dig through your backpack for that forgotten homework assignment, for the love of all things good, *do not stop in the middle of the hallway*. You're not the only one trying to get to class, and stopping in the middle of the flow of traffic is the equivalent of slamming on the brakes in the middle of a highway. Move to the side, find a quiet corner, and then do whatever you need to do. Your fellow students will thank you.

2. Walk on the Right Side
High school hallways are not the place to test out your rebellious streak by walking against the flow of traffic. Stick to the right side of the hallway, just like you would on the road. This simple rule keeps the traffic moving smoothly and prevents head-on collisions. And trust me, no one wants to be the person who accidentally bumps into someone carrying a full tray of cafeteria food.

3. Respect the Personal Bubble
In the crowded hallways of high school, personal space is a luxury. That said, it's still important to respect people's personal bubbles as much as possible. No one wants to feel like they're being herded like cattle, so try to give people a little breathing room. This rule is especially important when it comes to backpacks—if your backpack is so big that it's smacking people in the face as you walk by, it might be time to downsize.

4. Keep Conversations Moving
Yes, it's great to catch up with friends between classes, but the hallway is not the place for an in-depth conversation. If you stop in the middle of the hallway to have a chat with your friend, you're blocking the path for everyone else. If you need to talk, walk and talk. Just make sure you're watching where you're going!

Hallway Hazards: The Untold Dangers

Aside from the human obstacles, high school hallways are full of unexpected hazards. One of the most notorious is the slippery floor. Whether it's the result of a recently mopped hallway or a spilled soda, slippery floors are a disaster waiting to happen. There's nothing quite as embarrassing as wiping out in the middle of the hallway while everyone watches. It's the stuff of nightmares. You know the drill: one moment you're walking confidently, and the next, your feet are flying out from under you, and you're lying flat on your back, surrounded by concerned (and secretly amused) classmates.

Then, there's the backpack traffic jam. In high school, backpacks come in all shapes and sizes, but there's always that one person whose backpack is *way* too big. They take up the entire hallway as they walk, and heaven forbid they turn around quickly—you'll get smacked right in the face by a swinging backpack strap. Navigating the hallway around these oversized backpacks is like trying to maneuver through an obstacle course, except the obstacles are constantly moving.

And let's not forget the surprise pop quizzes. No, I'm not talking about academic quizzes—I'm talking about the surprise social interactions that pop up when you least expect them. You're walking down the hallway, minding your own business, when suddenly, someone you barely know stops to say hi. You panic, unsure whether you should stop and chat or keep walking. What's the appropriate length of a hallway conversation? How do you gracefully end it when you're already late to class? These are the real mysteries of the high school experience.

The Impossible Map: The Labyrinth of Hallways

Every high school has that one area of the building that defies all logic. It's the hallway that doesn't seem to lead anywhere or the stairwell that mysteriously skips a floor. It's as if the school architects decided to throw in a maze just for fun.

Imagine this: You're trying to find the library, and according to your map, it's on the second floor. So, you take the stairs up to the second floor, but when you get there, all you see are classrooms labeled with numbers you've never seen before. You try asking for directions, but no one seems to know where the library is either. You end up wandering aimlessly for what feels like hours, eventually stumbling upon a janitor's closet, but still no library.

High schools are full of these architectural mysteries. There's the hallway that loops back on itself, the classroom hidden behind an unmarked door, and the staircase that only certain teachers seem to know about. If you ever figure out the secret layout of your high school, consider yourself a genius. For the rest of us, navigating the hallways remains an unsolved puzzle.

Final Thoughts: Embrace the Chaos

Navigating the hallways of high school is an art form. It's chaotic, confusing, and occasionally dangerous, but it's also a rite of passage. From dodging slow walkers to surviving the hallway stampede, the high school hallway experience is one you'll never forget.

So, the next time you find yourself lost in the maze of hallways or trapped behind someone carrying a giant backpack, just remember: You're not alone. Every student has been there, and one day, you'll look back and laugh at the time you got stuck in the hallway intersection, desperately trying to get to class on time. Until then, embrace the chaos, and maybe invest in some good walking shoes.

Chapter 7: Group Projects—Or Group Torture?

Group projects. Two words that send shivers down the spine of high school students everywhere. On paper, they sound like a great idea—collaboration, teamwork, shared responsibility. But in reality, group projects are often anything but harmonious. What should be a collective effort to get a good grade can quickly spiral into chaos, leaving you either pulling your hair out in frustration or doing everything yourself to avoid disaster. In short, group projects can feel more like *group torture*.

In this chapter, we'll dive deep into the horrors and hilarity of high school group projects. From dealing with the inevitable slacker to trying to juggle conflicting schedules, we'll cover it all. And don't worry—we'll throw in some survival tips to help you avoid disaster and maintain your sanity (or at least what's left of it).

The Cast of Characters in Every Group Project

Before we dive into the specific challenges of group projects, let's meet the classic characters who always seem to show up in every group. Whether you're in biology, history, or English class, these roles remain surprisingly consistent.

1. The Overachiever
This person is the group's unofficial leader—and not always by choice. The overachiever is the student who takes charge, organizes everything, and makes sure the project gets done (even if it means doing most of the work themselves). They're the one sending late-night reminder texts, setting up meetings, and anxiously watching the deadline approach like a ticking time bomb. Often, their perfectionism drives them to take on more than their fair share, which is both a blessing and a curse for the rest of the group.

2. The Slacker
Ah, the slacker. The bane of every group project. This person contributes little to nothing and has a remarkable talent for disappearing just when it's time to actually do some work. Whether they're sleeping in the back of the

classroom or conveniently "forgetting" to show up for meetings, the slacker manages to coast along, often benefiting from the hard work of everyone else. Every group has one, and every group dreads it.

3. The Social Butterfly
The social butterfly may not be the hardest worker, but they're the life of the group—at least in terms of conversation. This person is more interested in chatting than actually getting the project done. They'll spend 20 minutes talking about weekend plans or the latest gossip, all while contributing very little to the project itself. They're fun to be around, sure, but when deadlines loom, you'll wish they'd stop talking and start working.

4. The Ghost
Similar to the slacker, the ghost is someone who is rarely seen or heard from during the project. They'll nod and smile during group discussions but never actually show up for any of the work. When you try to contact them for help, they're mysteriously unavailable. By the end of the project, you're left wondering if they even remember they were part of the group at all.

5. The Procrastinator
The procrastinator isn't necessarily lazy; they just love to leave everything until the last possible moment. They'll assure you, "Don't worry, I'll get it done," but their track record of starting assignments at midnight the day before it's due doesn't exactly inspire confidence. The procrastinator will eventually pull through, but their last-minute efforts can leave the group in a constant state of anxiety.

Now that we've met the cast of characters, let's look at the specific challenges these group dynamics create.

The "I'll Do It All Myself" Dilemma

If you've ever been the overachiever in a group project, you know the struggle. It's not that you *want* to do all the work—it's just that no one else seems capable of getting it done. You start out with good intentions, thinking, "We'll all work together, and this will be a team effort." But soon enough, you're staring at a blank Google Doc three days before the project is due, and the only person who's done anything is... well, you.

So, what do you do? You could wait for your group members to step up, but as the deadline approaches, your anxiety starts to skyrocket. Instead of risking a mediocre grade, you take matters into your own hands. You write the entire report, create the presentation, and even design the visuals— because someone has to.

By the time the project is submitted, you're exhausted and bitter, but hey, at least you got an A, right?

The "I'll do it all myself" dilemma is a common one, but it's important to recognize that taking on the entire workload isn't always the best solution. Sure, you might get the project done, but at the cost of your own mental health and well-being. Plus, it reinforces the idea that it's okay for the rest of the group to slack off, knowing you'll pick up the pieces.

The Slacker Struggle: Dealing with the Freeloader

Perhaps the most infuriating part of group projects is dealing with the slacker—the person who contributes nothing but still expects to get the same grade as everyone else. The slacker will come up with every excuse in the book to avoid work. "I'm really busy right now." "I had a family emergency." "I'll definitely help tomorrow." Spoiler alert: tomorrow never comes.

Trying to get the slacker to do their share is like pulling teeth. You send polite reminders, ask for their input, and try to assign them small, manageable tasks. But no matter what you do, they just don't come through. The worst part? When the project is finally finished, the slacker will smile and say, "We did great, didn't we?" *We*? Really?

One way to avoid the slacker struggle is to clearly assign roles from the very beginning. Set expectations early, and make sure everyone knows what they're responsible for. If the slacker still doesn't contribute, you'll have documentation to back you up if you need to talk to the teacher about redistributing the grades.

Another survival tip is to limit your emotional investment. Yes, it's frustrating when someone doesn't pull their weight, but stressing out over their lack of effort won't help you in the long run. Focus on doing your best and let the chips fall where they may. You can't control the slacker, but you can control how you respond.

The Nightmare of Scheduling Meetings

One of the most challenging parts of any group project is trying to find a time when everyone can meet. Between sports practices, extracurricular activities, part-time jobs, and social lives, it's nearly impossible to get everyone in the same room (or Zoom call) at the same time. The conversation usually goes something like this:

You: "Can we meet after school on Tuesday?"
Person 1: "I have soccer practice."
Person 2: "I work after school."
Person 3: "I can't—I'm volunteering that day."

And so it goes. Days pass, and you've still made zero progress on the project because no one can find a time to meet. By the time you finally agree on a time, it's 9 PM the night before the project is due, and everyone's panicking.

One solution to this problem is to embrace the power of technology. If you can't meet in person, use Google Docs, group chats, or video calls to collaborate remotely. Divide up the work and check in with each other online to make sure everyone is making progress. Sure, it's not as ideal as meeting face-to-face, but in the age of the internet, it's definitely doable.

Another tip is to set deadlines for individual tasks early on. If you know that scheduling a group meeting is going to be a nightmare, assign specific parts of the project to each person and set clear deadlines for when they need to submit their work. That way, you can assemble the project in pieces without relying on everyone being available at the same time.

The Hilarious Miscommunication

Group projects are full of miscommunication, and some of it is unintentionally hilarious. Maybe someone misunderstood the assignment and spent hours working on something completely unrelated. Or perhaps someone misinterpreted the instructions and showed up to present a totally different topic. Whatever the case, group projects are fertile ground for comedic errors.

Imagine this scenario: You're in charge of putting together the slides for the group presentation, and one of your teammates sends you their notes. But instead of getting detailed information, you receive a bulleted list of memes they thought would "lighten the mood" during the presentation. Or maybe you ask one of your group members to find supporting research, and they come back with a Wikipedia article they copied and pasted—complete with broken hyperlinks and citation needed tags.

These moments are frustrating, but sometimes all you can do is laugh. After all, high school group projects are as much about learning to work withothers as they are about the actual content.

Survival Tips for Group Projects

So how do you survive a group project without losing your mind? Here are some tips to help you navigate the chaos and come out on top:

1. Set Clear Expectations Early
Before you even start the project, make sure everyone knows their role and what they're responsible for. This will help avoid confusion and hold people accountable if they don't pull their weight.

2. Divide and Conquer
Break the project into smaller, manageable tasks and assign them to each group member. This way, no one feels overwhelmed, and it's easier to track progress.

3. Use Technology
If scheduling in-person meetings is a nightmare, use online tools to collaborate remotely. Google Docs, group chats, and video calls can be lifesavers when everyone's schedules conflict.

4. Set Mini Deadlines
Don't wait until the last minute to complete the project. Set smaller deadlines along the way so that everyone stays on track and the work gets done gradually.

5. Don't Be Afraid to Ask for Help
If you're really struggling with a slacker or a group that refuses to work together, don't hesitate to talk to your teacher. They'll likely have advice or be able to adjust the grading to reflect individual contributions.

Final Thoughts: Embrace the Chaos

Group projects are often a mess of conflicting schedules, uneven workloads, and miscommunication. But they're also a valuable learning experience that teaches you how to collaborate with others—even when it's frustrating. The next time you find yourself in the midst of a group project disaster, remember that you're not alone. Every student has survived the group project gauntlet, and so will you.

So embrace the chaos, do your best, and remember to laugh at the absurdity of it all. Because in the end, group projects aren't just about getting a grade—they're about learning how to work with people, and that's a skill you'll need long after high school.

Chapter 8: Social Media Mishaps

Social media is like a high school hallway that never sleeps—it's chaotic, full of drama, and even more awkward than the real thing. As if navigating high school wasn't already difficult enough, social media has added a whole new layer of complexity. In an age where every post, like, and comment is open to public scrutiny, it's no surprise that social media mishaps are bound to happen. Whether you're trying to impress your crush, keep up with the latest trends, or just survive without embarrassing yourself, social media is a minefield where one wrong move can lead to cringe-worthy disasters.

In this chapter, we'll explore the funny yet terrifying world of high school social media mishaps. From the classic accidental like to posting too soon and dealing with screenshot fails, we'll dive into the situations that send students into a spiral of embarrassment. And, of course, we'll give you some survival tips for making it through the digital drama unscathed—or at least with your dignity mostly intact.

Accidental Likes: The Ultimate Lurker's Nightmare

One of the most infamous social media mishaps is the accidental like. It's happened to all of us—you're casually lurking on someone's Instagram profile, doing your best detective work, and you're 35 weeks deep into their feed. You're trying to learn all about them without actually engaging, and that's when disaster strikes. Your finger slips, and before you know it, you've accidentally double-tapped a post from *months* ago. That's right, you've liked a post from the depths of their timeline, and there's no going back.

The accidental like is the ultimate horror because it exposes you as a lurker. Suddenly, that person knows you were creeping on their profile, and worse, they know you were scrolling through ancient history. You quickly unlike the post and pray they didn't get a notification, but let's be real—*they did*. Now they know, and you're left wondering if you should pack up and move to a different school to escape the shame.

What's the solution when you've committed the accidental like? There are a few strategies you can try.

1. **Panic and delete your entire Instagram account.** Okay, maybe this is a bit extreme, but in the heat of the moment, it feels like a valid option.
2. **Pretend it never happened.** If you quickly unliked the post, there's a chance they won't notice. Of course, this option comes with a high risk factor.
3. **Own it.** Send a casual message saying, "LOL, sorry, I didn't mean to like that post from 67 weeks ago. My bad!" It's embarrassing, sure, but it shows you can laugh at yourself, which might make the whole thing less awkward.

Accidental likes are a rite of passage in high school social media life. Everyone's done it at least once, and while it may feel like the most humiliating moment ever, the truth is that most people forget about it pretty quickly. Just don't make it a habit, and you'll survive.

Screenshot Fails: When Private Conversations Go Public

Another classic social media mishap is the screenshot fail, and trust me, this one can be even more mortifying than the accidental like. Screenshots are a standard tool in the high school gossip arsenal—you take a screenshot of a funny text, a drama-filled DM, or a questionable post, and you send it to your friends to dissect. But when you accidentally send the screenshot *to the person you were talking about*, things get awkward *real* fast.

Imagine this: Your friend posts something ridiculous on their Instagram story, and you can't help but share it with your group chat for a good laugh. You screenshot it and send it… but in your haste, you accidentally send it to the *person who posted it*. Cue immediate panic. There's no smooth way out of this one. You've just been caught talking behind their back, and there's no undoing it.

How do you recover from a screenshot fail?

1. **Play dumb.** "Oops! That wasn't meant for you!" While this won't erase the fact that you were clearly talking about them, it can diffuse some of the tension.

2. **Apologize.** Own up to the mistake and apologize for the awkwardness. Depending on the severity of the situation, a sincere apology can go a long way.
3. **Ghost them.** If all else fails, disappear into the digital abyss. Stop replying, stop posting, and maybe take a brief break from social media until the dust settles.

The lesson here? Always double-check before sending a screenshot. In the world of high school social media, one wrong click can turn your private joke into public humiliation.

The Dangers of Posting Too Soon: Social Media Regret

We've all experienced that rush of excitement when we think we've captured the perfect photo or come up with the funniest caption. In that moment, it feels like the world needs to see it *right now*. But here's the thing: posting too soon can often lead to serious social media regret.

Maybe you posted a photo you thought was cute, only to realize minutes later that your hair was doing something weird or your smile looked more like a grimace. Or perhaps you shared a status update about how excited you are for a new relationship, only for things to go south the very next day. Suddenly, that adorable post feels like a ticking time bomb of embarrassment.

Posting too soon is especially dangerous in high school, where trends, opinions, and relationships change at lightning speed. What seemed like a good idea in the moment can quickly become the source of ridicule when circumstances change.

The best way to avoid social media regret? Follow the 24-hour rule. If you're unsure about a post, give it a day. Sleep on it. If you still feel good about it the next day, go ahead and share it. But if you wake up with second thoughts, you've saved yourself from some potential awkwardness.

Also, remember that you can always delete a post. Sure, someone might have screenshotted it, but it's better to delete it and deal with a few jokes than to let your cringe-worthy post live forever on the internet.

The Curse of the Typo: It's Always Worse Online

Typos are bad enough in regular texts, but when they happen on social media, they feel a hundred times worse. That witty caption you spent 10 minutes crafting? Ruined by a misplaced apostrophe or a misspelled word.

And because it's social media, everyone *sees* it. Even worse, some people will delight in pointing it out.

Typos on social media are a nightmare because they can completely change the meaning of what you were trying to say. You were trying to be funny, but instead, you accidentally wrote something nonsensical or, worse, offensive. Cue the flood of comments calling out your mistake.

The best way to avoid this? Always proofread before you post. Double-check your spelling, punctuation, and grammar to make sure everything looks right. If you're unsure about something, ask a friend to take a look before it goes live. And if you do make a mistake, don't panic—most platforms let you edit your posts, so you can quickly fix it before too many people notice.

Of course, if it's too late and the typo is already out in the wild, just laugh it off. Typos happen to the best of us, and the more you own it, the less people will make fun of you for it.

DM Disasters: Messaging Gone Wrong

Direct messages (DMs) are where a lot of the real high school social media drama happens. Whether you're sliding into someone's DMs to strike up a conversation with your crush or hashing out the latest drama with your best friend, DMs are a digital minefield. One wrong move can lead to some seriously awkward moments.

The most common DM disaster? Sending a message to the wrong person. You're typing out a long, emotional message about how annoyed you are with someone, but instead of sending it to your best friend, you accidentally send it to the *person you're complaining about*. Ouch.

Or maybe you're trying to flirt with your crush, but you send the message to a completely different person—maybe even a teacher or a relative. It's the kind of mistake that makes you want to throw your phone out the window and pretend it never happened.

To avoid DM disasters, always double-check who you're sending a message to before you hit send. It's also a good idea to keep your messages short and sweet—long, detailed rants are more likely to end in embarrassment if sent to the wrong person. If you do mess up, apologize immediately and try to laugh it off. Everyone makes mistakes, and the more you can roll with the punches, the less painful it will be.

The Eternal Fear: Being Left on Read

In the world of high school social media, nothing is worse than being left on read. You send a DM, and you can see that the other person has opened it—but they don't respond. The minutes tick by, then hours, and you're left wondering what went wrong. Did you say something weird? Are they mad at you? Are they ghosting you?

The truth is, being left on read is one of the most common (and most painful) social media experiences. It leaves you feeling vulnerable and unsure of yourself. But here's the thing: it doesn't always mean what you think it does. Sometimes people get busy, forget to respond, or don't know how to reply. It doesn't automatically mean they're ignoring you.

The best way to deal with being left on read? Don't take it personally. People have their own lives and their own reasons for not responding right away. If it's been a few days and you're still anxious, send a follow-up message. If they still don't respond, it's time to move on and focus on other friendships.

Surviving Social Media in High School: A Survival Guide

High school social media is full of potential pitfalls, but it's also a place for fun, connection, and self-expression. To survive—and even thrive—online during your high school years, here are a few key tips:

1. **Double-check everything** before you post, send, or screenshot. It'll save you from countless embarrassing situations.
2. **Don't take yourself too seriously.** Everyone makes mistakes online, and the more you can laugh at your own social media mishaps, the better you'll feel.
3. **Give yourself breaks** from social media when it starts to feel overwhelming. It's easy to get caught up in the drama, but taking time to step away can help you keep your perspective.
4. **Think before you post.** If you're unsure about a post, wait 24 hours. It might save you from some serious regret later on.
5. **Remember that social media isn't real life.** It's easy to compare yourself to others online, but what you see on social media is only a small piece of the puzzle. Everyone has their own struggles, whether or not they post about them.

In the end, social media is what you make of it. Sure, there will be some embarrassing moments along the way, but with a little humor and a lot of caution, you can make it through the online world with your dignity intact.

Chapter 9: The Awkward School Dance

The school dance: a rite of passage for every high school student, promising an evening filled with excitement, mystery, and—let's be real—awkwardness. It's the one night where the whole school comes together to celebrate… something. The theme doesn't even matter because the focus of the night is always the same: avoiding embarrassment while trying to have a good time. And no matter how many school dances you attend, there's always the inevitable combination of bad dance moves, cringe-worthy outfit choices, and awkward social interactions that make you wonder why you even showed up in the first place.

But here's the secret no one tells you: the awkwardness is what makes school dances fun! It's not about being the best dancer or having the trendiest outfit. It's about surviving the night with a sense of humor and embracing the fact that *everyone* feels just as awkward as you do.

In this chapter, we'll explore the highs and lows of the school dance experience—from the painful build-up to the post-dance gossip—and offer some tips on how to laugh off the cringe-worthy moments and make the most of the ultimate social event of the year.

The Build-up: Planning for the "Big Night"

The drama of the school dance starts long before the actual event. Weeks in advance, the buzz begins to spread throughout the school. "Who's going with who?" "What's the theme this year?" "Will I actually be brave enough to ask my crush to dance?" These are the questions that dominate every lunch table conversation, group chat, and hallway whisper.

For most students, the build-up is half the experience. You spend hours agonizing over what to wear, overthinking every little detail like it's a red carpet event at the Oscars. Should you go with a dress that screams *sophisticated elegance* or one that says *I casually threw this together*? If you're a guy, do you go for the classic button-down shirt and tie combo, or do you aim for a "cool but casual" vibe with sneakers and a blazer? It doesn't really matter because, in the end, it's impossible to strike the perfect balance between looking cool and trying too hard.

Then, there's the matter of your "date." For some, asking someone to the dance feels like a high-stakes operation, complete with rehearsed lines and backup plans in case of rejection. For others, it's a no-pressure group outing where everyone's just happy to be there. Either way, the pressure builds as the day of the dance approaches, and you're left wondering if it will live up to the expectations you've created in your head. Spoiler alert: it never does, but that's part of the charm.

The Grand Entrance: Awkward From the Start

Fast forward to the night of the dance. You've spent hours getting ready, your outfit is on point (or so you think), and you've finally arrived at the school gymnasium, which has been transformed into a dance floor, complete with balloons, streamers, and a DJ who's already playing music that no one will actually dance to for at least another hour.

The first awkward moment happens right at the entrance. As you and your friends walk in, you're met with the harsh reality that no one is dancing yet. Instead, everyone is standing in small groups, nervously chatting and pretending to be too cool to care. It's like a high school social experiment— everyone is waiting for someone else to start dancing first, but no one wants to be the brave soul who breaks the ice.

If you're really unlucky, the dance has a photo booth, and somehow, you get roped into taking a group photo before you even step foot on the dance floor. This results in a series of awkward poses and forced smiles, as you try to figure out whether to go for a serious face or just embrace the ridiculousness of it all. Either way, you'll be haunted by these photos for years to come when they inevitably end up in the yearbook.

The Dance Floor Dilemma: To Dance or Not to Dance

Eventually, the DJ plays a song that's catchy enough to get a few brave souls to hit the dance floor, and the crowd slowly starts to trickle in. But now comes the big question: *Do you dance?* For some, dancing is a natural instinct. For others, it's an awkward, self-conscious activity where every movement feels like you're being judged by the entire room.

The key to surviving the dance floor dilemma is to embrace the awkwardness. No one is expecting you to bust out professional dance moves or perfectly nail the latest TikTok trends. In fact, the more ridiculous your dance moves, the better. Think of it as an opportunity to channel your inner "dad at a wedding" energy. You know the moves—the classic finger guns, the two-step shuffle, and maybe even a poorly timed attempt at the moonwalk. The point is to have fun, not to impress.

For those who are really feeling brave, there's always the possibility of a slow dance. But let's be honest, slow dances are the epitome of awkward. First, you've got to figure out if anyone wants to dance with you. Then, if you do find a partner, there's the delicate balancing act of how close to stand, where to put your hands, and whether or not to make eye contact. It's a high school rite of passage, but it's also the kind of experience that makes you want to cringe and laugh at the same time.

Outfit Disasters: When Things Don't Go as Planned

Every school dance has at least one wardrobe malfunction waiting to happen. Whether it's a dress that's a little too long and causes a tripping hazard or a tie that refuses to stay straight, outfit disasters are as much a part of the dance experience as the music and lights.

One of the classic high school dance mishaps is wearing shoes that look amazing but are impossible to walk in. You thought those heels or fancy dress shoes would complete your outfit, but after just 15 minutes of standing around, your feet are begging for mercy. Suddenly, your only goal for the night is finding the nearest chair and staying off the dance floor altogether.

For others, the disaster comes in the form of an ill-fitting outfit. Maybe that dress or suit seemed like a good idea in the store, but now that you're at the dance, it feels too tight, too loose, or just all-around uncomfortable. You spend the entire night pulling at your clothes, trying to readjust while hoping no one notices your discomfort.

But here's the good news: no one else is paying attention to your wardrobe mishap because they're too busy worrying about their own. The secret to surviving an outfit disaster? Laugh it off. If you trip over your own shoes or accidentally spill punch on your shirt, just roll with it. The more you can laugh at yourself, the more fun you'll have.

The Snack Table: A Social Safe Haven

When the dance floor becomes too overwhelming, there's always one place you can retreat to: the snack table. It's the social safe haven of every school dance—the one place where you can take a break from the awkwardness of dancing and socialize over cookies, chips, and mystery punch that no one can quite identify.

The snack table is also where some of the best people-watching happens. From a distance, you can observe the dance floor antics without having to be directly involved. You'll witness everything from wild dance moves to awkward slow dances, all while happily munching on a cookie and feeling grateful for the brief respite from the social pressures of the dance floor.

And let's not forget the social dynamics of the snack table itself. Inevitably, you'll run into people who are doing the exact same thing as you—avoiding the dance floor—and it becomes a kind of unspoken club of snack table dwellers. You bond over your shared love of free food and your mutual desire to avoid public embarrassment, and before you know it, the awkwardness of the night starts to fade away.

The Post-Dance Analysis: What Really Happened?

After the dance, the real fun begins: the post-dance analysis. This is when you and your friends rehash every moment of the night, from the music choices to the most awkward encounters. Who danced with who? Who made a fool of themselves on the dance floor? Who had the best (and worst) outfit? These are the important questions that dominate the conversation for days afterward.

No matter how awkward or embarrassing the dance was, the post-dance analysis is where the night becomes legendary. Suddenly, all those cringe-worthy moments don't seem so bad—they're just funny stories to laugh about with your friends. The key to surviving the school dance is remembering that it's not about perfection. It's about making memories, even if those memories involve tripping over your own feet or wearing a dress that felt like a straightjacket.

Tips for Surviving (and Enjoying) the Awkward School Dance

So how do you make the most of the school dance experience without letting the awkwardness ruin your night? Here are a few tips:

1. **Embrace the Awkwardness.** Everyone feels awkward at school dances, so you might as well lean into it. Laugh at your own dance moves, don't take yourself too seriously, and remember that no one is judging you as much as you think they are.

2. **Wear Something Comfortable.** Sure, you want to look good, but make sure you can actually move (and breathe) in your outfit. If your shoes are killing you, ditch them and dance barefoot—no one will care.

3. **Don't Wait to Dance.** Don't waste half the night standing around waiting for someone else to start dancing. Get out there early and have fun, even if you're just doing the sprinkler in the corner with your friends.

4. **Use the Snack Table to Your Advantage.** The snack table is a great place to take a break, refuel, and socialize without the pressure of dancing. Plus, free food is always a win.

5. **Focus on Fun, Not Perfection.** The school dance is not a life-or-death event. It's just one night, and it's meant to be fun. Don't stress about every little detail—just go with the flow and enjoy the ride.

In the end, the awkwardness is what makes school dances memorable. Years from now, you won't remember whether or not your outfit was perfect or if your dance moves were flawless. What you'll remember are the laughs, the awkward moments, and the stories that you'll tell for years to come. So embrace the cringe, have fun, and remember that the awkward school dance is a rite of passage—one that you'll survive with a sense of humor and a lot of great memories.

Chapter 10: Test Day Terror

There are few things more universally feared in high school than test days. Whether it's a surprise pop quiz, the dreaded midterm, or the looming specter of standardized tests, the sheer terror that comes with exam season is unmatched. It doesn't matter how well you've been doing in class—test day has a way of making even the most prepared students break out into a cold sweat. It's a high-pressure gauntlet of multiple-choice questions, essay prompts, and fill-in-the-blanks designed to make you question not only what you've learned, but also your very existence.

But fear not! Test days, while terrifying, are also ripe with opportunities for humor. In this chapter, we'll explore the horrors of test day, the funny mishaps that come with it, and how to survive exam season without losing your mind—or your dignity.

Pop Quiz Panic: The Definition of Unfair

Let's start with the ultimate act of academic betrayal: the pop quiz. There's nothing quite like the sinking feeling you get when you walk into class, ready for a normal day, and your teacher announces, "Surprise! Pop quiz!" It's the educational equivalent of being ambushed by ninjas—totally unexpected and designed to leave you feeling helpless and confused.

You're immediately hit with a wave of panic as your mind races to recall *anything* that was mentioned in class over the last week. You start flipping through mental flashcards, trying to remember obscure facts that were only mentioned once during a lecture. It's amazing how quickly your brain goes blank when faced with a pop quiz, as if all your knowledge has evaporated the moment you need it the most.

Then there's the awkward glances exchanged between classmates. You look around, hoping to catch someone else's eye who might be just as clueless as you. There's usually that one student who *did* study, sitting confidently at the front of the room, while the rest of the class collectively descends into chaos.

If you're really unlucky, the pop quiz is multiple-choice, which means you're forced to engage in the classic "guessing game." You stare at the four options, knowing deep down that at least two of them are there just to mess with your head. You start using absurd logic to make your choice: "Well, I haven't picked 'C' in a while, so it must be the answer."

Survival tip: When faced with a pop quiz, the best strategy is to stay calm and do your best. If all else fails, embrace the guessing game and remember that it's just one quiz—your academic future doesn't hinge on whether or not you know the exact date of the Treaty of Versailles.

Midterms: The Week from Hell

While pop quizzes are scary in their unpredictability, midterms are terrifying for the exact opposite reason. You know they're coming, you know what they'll cover, and yet the panic sets in days (or weeks) in advance. Midterms are like the academic equivalent of a horror movie where the monster is slowly creeping up on you, and no matter how hard you try to prepare, you never feel quite ready.

The days leading up to midterms are filled with an endless stream of study sessions, flashcards, and half-hearted attempts to explain complex concepts to yourself in front of a mirror. Suddenly, everything you learned in the first half of the year feels like it's been wiped from your brain. You start questioning how you managed to survive this long in school without understanding basic algebra or remembering key historical dates.

One of the funniest parts of midterm week is the overconfidence of the "totally forgot to study" student. This person boldly announces, "I didn't even study, but I'm sure I'll do fine," only to have their confidence evaporate as soon as they sit down with the test in front of them. You can practically see the gears turning in their head as they realize they're in way over their head.

Of course, no midterm week is complete without at least one classmate pulling an all-nighter. This is the student who shows up to the exam with dark circles under their eyes and a gallon-sized coffee cup in hand, claiming they crammed all night. Spoiler alert: this strategy rarely works. By the time the test rolls around, their brain is so fried that they can barely remember their own name, let alone the key themes of *Romeo and Juliet*.

Survival tip: For midterms, preparation is key. Start studying early, break the material into manageable chunks, and avoid pulling all-nighters (seriously, they're not worth it). And if you feel unprepared, remind yourself that everyone is just as nervous as you are. Midterms are stressful, but they're also a great way to practice pacing yourself and learning how to study effectively.

The Standardized Test Struggle: Why Does This Even Exist?

If there's one type of test that strikes fear into the hearts of all high school students, it's the standardized test. These tests are supposed to measure your academic abilities, but let's be real—they mostly measure how well you can sit still for three hours without losing your mind.

From the SAT to the ACT to the endless parade of state-mandated assessments, standardized tests feel like a cruel joke. They're designed to cover a wide range of topics, many of which you probably haven't studied in years (geometry, anyone?). And don't even get me started on the reading comprehension section, which seems to consist of the most boring passages known to humanity.

One of the biggest challenges of standardized tests is pacing yourself. You start out strong, tackling the first few questions with confidence, but by the time you're halfway through, your brain feels like it's turned to mush. The clock is ticking, and suddenly you're faced with a math problem that looks like it's written in another language. You start doing mental gymnastics, trying to figure out if it's better to guess or skip it entirely.

Of course, standardized tests also come with their own unique set of distractions. There's always that one person who's furiously tapping their pencil against the desk, another who seems to be clearing their throat every five seconds, and someone who keeps asking to go to the bathroom. It's like a test of your focus and patience as much as your academic skills.

And let's not forget the post-test ritual: the moment you walk out of the testing room, everyone starts comparing answers. It's a race to see who remembered what, and inevitably, you'll hear someone say, "Wait, was the answer to question 12 *B*? Because I put *A*." Cue the sinking feeling in your stomach as you realize you may have bombed that question.

Survival tip: When it comes to standardized tests, practice is your best friend. Take practice tests, familiarize yourself with the format, and try not to get too caught up in the pressure. It's easy to feel overwhelmed, but remember that these tests don't define your worth as a student or a person.

Funny Test Day Stories: The "Totally Forgot to Study" Crowd

Every test day comes with its own set of hilarious stories, and most of them involve that one classmate who "totally forgot to study." You know the type—the person who strolls into the classroom on test day with zero preparation, acting as if they'll somehow ace the exam through sheer luck or charm.

One classic move is the "desperate last-minute cramming session." This person shows up five minutes before the test starts, frantically flipping through their notes as if they can absorb weeks' worth of material in a few short minutes. You can practically see the panic on their face as they try to memorize key terms while the teacher hands out the test papers.

Then there's the "confidence facade." This student will sit down at their desk and loudly proclaim, "I didn't study, but I'm sure I'll do fine." Of course, this confidence quickly fades once the test begins, and they realize they don't know the answer to the first five questions. By the end of the test, they're filling in random answers and praying for a miracle.

One of my personal favorite test day mishaps is the "creative answer" strategy. When you don't know the answer to a question, sometimes the best you can do is throw in a wild guess or write something ridiculous just to amuse yourself (and maybe the teacher). For example, if you don't know the date of the Battle of Hastings, you might as well guess "1842" and add a little doodle of a sword for good measure. Who knows? Maybe you'll get extra credit for creativity.

Strategies for Surviving Exam Season Without Losing Your Mind

Now that we've covered the horrors (and humor) of test day, let's talk about how to survive exam season without losing your mind.

1.   **Start Early**: It sounds obvious, but the earlier you start studying, the less stressful it will be. Break your study sessions into manageable chunks so you're not cramming the night before.

2. **Find Your Study Style**: Everyone learns differently. Whether it's making flashcards, studying with friends, or teaching yourself out loud, find what works best for you and stick to it.

3. **Take Breaks**: Studying for hours on end without a break is a recipe for burnout. Take short breaks to refresh your brain and keep your energy up.

4. **Get Plenty of Sleep**: Don't underestimate the power of a good night's sleep before a big test. You'll think more clearly and perform better if you're well-rested.

5. **Laugh It Off**: Test day is stressful, but it's also full of funny moments. If you make a mistake or bomb a question, don't dwell on it—just laugh it off and move on. No one's perfect, and everyone has their own test day horror stories.

Final Thoughts: Test Day Isn't the End of the World

Test days can feel like the ultimate nightmare, but in the grand scheme of things, they're just a small part of the high school experience. Whether it's a pop quiz, a midterm, or a standardized test, remember that everyone is in the same boat—nervous, stressed, and probably winging it a little. So, the next time you find yourself staring down a test paper with a mix of terror and confusion, take a deep breath, relax, and remind yourself that you'll survive—*and* you'll probably have a funny story to tell when it's all over.

Chapter 11: Parent-Teacher Conference Nightmares

Parent-teacher conference night is one of those events that strikes fear into the heart of every high school student. Sure, it sounds like a simple, routine evening where parents and teachers meet to discuss your academic progress. But in reality, it's an anxiety-inducing gauntlet where every embarrassing detail of your school life could be revealed in a matter of minutes. It's like having your entire high school existence put under a microscope, with your parents and teachers analyzing every flaw and weakness.

From the dread of walking into school with your parents to the sheer terror of wondering what your teachers are going to reveal, parent-teacher conference night can feel like a nightmare come to life. And let's not forget the awkward moments when your teachers share stories about things you *thought* no one noticed. Suddenly, all those side glances, whispered comments, and quiet daydreams during class are exposed for everyone to see.

But as terrifying as parent-teacher conference night can be, it's also full of hilarious moments. In this chapter, we'll explore the panic, the awkwardness, and the unintentional comedy that comes with watching your parents and teachers meet. Plus, we'll offer some survival tips on how to prepare for this annual event and maybe even come out of it unscathed.

The Build-Up: A Week of Dread

The panic starts long before the actual parent-teacher conference night. In the days leading up to the event, you know it's coming. You start to notice the reminders from your teachers: "Don't forget, parent-teacher conferences are this Thursday!" It's like they're reminding you of an unavoidable doom. You see the notices pinned to classroom walls, hear whispers in the hallways, and feel the rising tension as your classmates begin to exchange nervous glances.

You start mentally reviewing every interaction you've had with your teachers, wondering if they'll mention that one time you accidentally fell asleep in class, or worse, the time you got caught passing notes to your friend. You try to remember if you turned in that last assignment on time or if you've participated enough to avoid the dreaded label of "could try harder."

Then, you begin the delicate task of prepping your parents. You know they're going to ask questions—about your grades, your behavior, and why you've been coming home with crumpled worksheets stuffed in your backpack. And while you'd love for them to walk in with zero expectations and zero questions, that's never the case. So, you start offering vague, carefully curated information about your teachers. "Oh, Mrs. Johnson? Yeah, she's super nice. Really chill. She'll probably say I'm doing fine. Mr. Andrews? Well, he's kind of strict, but don't worry, I'm definitely keeping up in his class."

The goal is simple: give your parents just enough information to keep them calm, but not so much that they start getting curious or (heaven forbid) *involved*. You want them to go in with minimal expectations and come out thinking you're a model student, even if that's not quite the case.

The Walk of Doom: Entering the Conference

Parent-teacher conference night arrives, and the dread settles in. You walk into the school with your parents, feeling like you're marching toward an inevitable disaster. The school, which is normally bustling with students, now feels oddly quiet, as if the building itself knows something ominous is about to happen.

As you enter the gym or the cafeteria (depending on where the conferences are being held), you're immediately hit with a wave of tension. You can see your fellow students sitting with their parents at small tables, looking anywhere but at their teachers. Some look confident, as if they know they've aced every test and assignment. Others, like you, are fidgeting nervously, trying to prepare for whatever embarrassing revelation might be coming next.

Your teachers sit behind long tables, looking far more approachable than they do during class, which only makes the whole situation feel even more surreal. It's like being in a weird alternate universe where teachers are smiling and asking parents how their day has been, but you know it's just a front before they start listing your academic shortcomings.

And then it happens: your parents and your teachers meet.

The Horror Stories: When Teachers Share Too Much

The worst part of parent-teacher conference night is the moment your teacher starts talking. You sit there, quietly cringing as they reveal details about your behavior, your habits, and your performance in class that you *really* didn't want your parents to know about.

Let's start with the embarrassing habits. Maybe you've been doodling in your notebook instead of taking notes during class. Or maybe you've been caught zoning out during long lectures. Whatever the case, your teacher will bring it up in the most cheerful, casual way possible, as if it's no big deal. "Oh, yes, Johnny's been quite creative in class lately—always drawing in his notebook! But, you know, we'd love for him to pay a little more attention during lessons."

Meanwhile, you're sitting there, mortified, as your parents shoot you that *look*. You know the one—the look that says, "We'll talk about this when we get home." You want to disappear into the floor, but instead, you're forced to nod along and pretend you had no idea that your teacher even noticed.

Then, there are the times when your teacher reveals that one embarrassing moment you thought had been forgotten. Maybe it was that time you knocked over your water bottle in the middle of class, spilling it all over your desk. Or maybe it was the day you got caught whispering to your friend during a quiz. "Yes, there was that one incident where Sarah got a little distracted during class, but she quickly got back on track!" Your parents chuckle, but you know that this story is going to be brought up at every family gathering for the next decade.

The Over-Achiever Friend Comparison

No parent-teacher conference night would be complete without the inevitable comparison to *that* student. You know who I'm talking about—the overachiever who sits at the front of the class, always raises their hand, and gets straight A's without even breaking a sweat. The worst part? That student is usually your friend.

Your teacher, with the best of intentions, will bring up this friend as a shining example of academic excellence. "You know, it's wonderful to see Johnny working alongside Sarah. She's always so focused and engaged in class—it really sets a great example for everyone!" And just like that, your parents' eyes light up. They turn to you with a look that clearly says, "Why can't you be more like Sarah?"

You try to sink lower in your chair, avoiding eye contact as your teacher continues to sing your friend's praises. It's not that you don't like Sarah—you do! She's great! But you don't need to be reminded of her greatness while your own less-than-stellar academic performance is being dissected in front of your parents.

Survival tip: When the comparison game starts, nod along, smile politely, and remind your parents later that not everyone is destined to be a straight-A student. After all, you have your own unique strengths—like your ability to come up with creative excuses for why you didn't finish your homework.

The Aftermath: The Car Ride Home

Once the conference is over, the real fun begins: the car ride home. If the conference went well, your parents will be all smiles, congratulating you on your hard work and maybe even offering to get you ice cream as a reward. But if the conference revealed a few too many embarrassing details, the car ride home becomes an awkward, silent journey where you can feel the disappointment radiating from the front seat.

You sit there, staring out the window, mentally preparing yourself for the inevitable lecture that's coming. Your parents will start out with the usual questions: "Why didn't you tell us you were falling behind in math?" or "How come your teacher said you're not paying attention in class?" You offer vague answers, trying to deflect the blame onto the *unreasonably* hard tests, or the fact that the teacher's explanations "just don't make sense."

Then, your parents move into the "motivation speech" portion of the evening, telling you how important it is to take school seriously and how they "just want what's best for you." You nod along, half-listening as you wonder how long it will take for this whole ordeal to blow over.

Survival Tips for Parent-Teacher Conference Night

Surviving parent-teacher conference night is all about preparation and damage control. Here are a few tips to help you navigate this nerve-wracking event with minimal embarrassment:

1. **Prep Your Parents in Advance**: Give your parents a heads-up about what your teachers might say. It's better to control the narrative than to be caught off guard. Let them know if you've been struggling

in a particular subject or if there's been any "minor" incidents in class.

2. **Build a Rapport with Your Teachers**: If you can, make a good impression on your teachers before conference night. That way, they'll be more likely to focus on the positives during the meeting. Be respectful, participate in class, and try not to give them any *too* embarrassing stories to share.

3. **Stay Calm and Collected**: Remember, the conference is just a small part of your overall high school experience. Even if your teachers reveal some embarrassing moments, it's not the end of the world. Stay calm, smile, and remind yourself that it'll all be over soon.

4. **Embrace the Humor**: Parent-teacher conferences are full of awkward moments, but they're also pretty funny when you think about it. Your parents meeting your teachers and dissecting your school life is an inherently strange experience. So, laugh it off and remember that one day, these cringe-worthy moments will be funny stories you can tell your friends.

Final Thoughts: Embrace the Awkwardness

Parent-teacher conference night may feel like a nightmare, but it's also a rite of passage. Every student has gone through the panic, the embarrassment, and the awkward conversations that come with watching your parents and teachers meet. But the truth is, it's never as bad as you think it's going to be. Sure, there might be a few cringe-worthy moments, but at the end of the day, your parents are just trying to understand what's going on in your academic life—and your teachers are just trying to help.

So, the next time parent-teacher conference night rolls around, take a deep breath, prepare your parents, and embrace the awkwardness. Because no matter what happens, you'll survive—and you'll probably have a funny story to tell when it's all over.

Chapter 12: The Quirks of High School Teachers

High school teachers are a special breed. They're the gatekeepers of knowledge, the enforcers of rules, and, more often than not, the stars of their own quirky little universes. Every student has encountered that one teacher who stands out, not just because they're good at what they do, but because of their weird and wonderful habits. Whether it's the teacher who wears the same sweater every day or the one who seems to take joy in handing out pop quizzes at the worst possible moments, these quirks are what make teachers memorable—and often, unintentionally hilarious.

In this chapter, we're going to dive into the eccentricities that make high school teachers so unique. From their wardrobe choices to their peculiar classroom rituals, you'll see why these teachers are impossible to forget. Plus, we'll throw in some funny dialogues and interactions between students and teachers that will leave you laughing, even if you've experienced these moments in real life.

The Sweater Teacher

There's always that one teacher who, no matter the season, weather, or occasion, wears the exact same sweater. Whether it's a trusty cardigan that looks like it's been through the wringer or a turtleneck that never seems to leave their body, this teacher is as loyal to their sweater as they are to their curriculum.

Mr. Thompson, for example, was famous for his navy-blue sweater that he wore every single day. It didn't matter if it was freezing cold or blistering hot —Mr. Thompson's sweater was a constant. Rumor had it that he owned multiple versions of the same sweater, and some students even speculated that he had a closet full of identical navy sweaters, one for each day of the week.

During one particularly warm spring, when the classroom AC wasn't working, a brave student decided to ask the question that had been on everyone's minds for years:

Student: "Mr. Thompson, isn't it a little hot for a sweater today?"

Mr. Thompson: (pausing mid-lecture) "Ah, you'd think so, wouldn't you? But this sweater has magical powers. It keeps me warm in the winter and cool in the summer."

The class erupted into laughter, but no one ever got a straight answer as to why Mr. Thompson refused to part with his beloved sweater. It was just one of those quirks you had to accept—and perhaps even admire. After all, anyone who can survive in a sweater during a 90-degree heatwave has earned some respect.

The Pop Quiz Master

If there's one thing high school students universally dread, it's the pop quiz. But for some teachers, pop quizzes aren't just a teaching tool—they're a way of life. Enter Ms. Jenkins, the Pop Quiz Master. Her quizzes were the stuff of legend, not because they were particularly hard (though they often were), but because they struck at the most unexpected moments.

Ms. Jenkins had an uncanny ability to time her pop quizzes perfectly, usually when the class was least prepared. The day after a school dance? Pop quiz. The morning after a big game when half the class was bleary-eyed from staying up late? Pop quiz. It became a running joke among students that Ms. Jenkins had a sixth sense for student exhaustion.

One day, after a particularly grueling week of tests in other classes, the students sat down in Ms. Jenkins' class, hoping for a break. She started the lesson as usual, lecturing about the causes of World War I, when suddenly, she paused and smiled—a smile that sent chills down everyone's spine.

Ms. Jenkins: "Alright, everyone, put your books away. It's time for a pop quiz!"

Student: (groaning) "But we just had a quiz last week!"

Ms. Jenkins: (grinning) "Yes, but you didn't have this quiz last week."

The class collectively sighed, knowing they were in for yet another surprise test. Over time, Ms. Jenkins' pop quizzes became legendary, and students learned to always be on their toes. After all, you never knew when the next one would strike.

The Random Fact Enthusiast

Some teachers are deeply passionate about their subjects. Others, however, seem to be passionate about *everything*—to the point where they can't help but bombard students with random facts, even if those facts have absolutely nothing to do with the lesson at hand.

Mr. Garcia, the history teacher, was one such educator. His love for trivia was boundless, and while his classes were supposed to be about historical events, they often turned into mini TED Talks on the most bizarre subjects. One minute, he'd be talking about the Industrial Revolution, and the next, he'd be explaining how octopuses have three hearts.

Mr. Garcia: "Now, let's get back to discussing the effects of the Industrial Revolution on society. Oh, and did you know that wombats poop in cubes?"

The students, used to Mr. Garcia's tangents, learned to expect the unexpected. Some even started keeping a tally of how many random facts he'd drop during each class.

Student: "Uh, Mr. Garcia, what does that have to do with the lesson?"

Mr. Garcia: (smiling) "Nothing at all, but isn't it fascinating? Alright, back to the Revolution!"

It didn't matter that half of the facts Mr. Garcia shared were completely unrelated to the curriculum. What mattered was that he made learning interesting—if not a little chaotic. His love for random trivia made him one of the most memorable teachers in the school, and students often found themselves sharing his random facts with their friends long after class had ended.

The Overly Enthusiastic Coach

While most teachers have a healthy level of excitement about their subject, some take enthusiasm to a whole new level—especially when that subject is physical education. Coach Stevens was a prime example of this. He approached every gym class as if it were the Olympics, and his energy was unmatched.

It didn't matter if you were running laps, playing dodgeball, or simply doing stretches—Coach Stevens treated every activity like it was the most important thing you'd ever do in your life. His voice boomed across the gym as he barked encouragements (and sometimes unintentionally hilarious insults) at students who were clearly not as enthusiastic about physical fitness as he was.

Coach Stevens: "Come on, Johnson! You can run faster than that! You've got legs—use them!"

Student: (barely jogging) "I'm trying, Coach!"

Coach Stevens: "Try harder! Picture yourself being chased by a pack of wild dogs! MOVE!"

His passion for fitness was admirable, but not everyone shared his excitement. For most students, gym class was a time to go through the motions and maybe sneak in some gossip between exercises. But for Coach Stevens, it was life or death.

Despite his intensity, students couldn't help but love Coach Stevens. His over-the-top enthusiasm made every class feel like an event, and even if you weren't exactly athletic, you couldn't help but admire his dedication to making gym class the highlight of your day—or at least, a day you'd never forget.

The Technology-Resistant Teacher

In the age of smartphones and smartboards, most teachers have adapted to the new world of technology. But then, there are those teachers who seem to be permanently stuck in the past, resisting every modern convenience. Mrs. Perkins, the English teacher, was one such example.

While the rest of the school had transitioned to using laptops and online submissions, Mrs. Perkins clung to her overhead projector like it was a lifeline. She loved using transparencies, and every day, she'd wheel out the dusty old projector to display hand-written notes that were barely legible.

Student: "Mrs. Perkins, why don't we just use the smartboard?"

Mrs. Perkins: (frowning) "Oh, those newfangled gadgets? No thank you. This projector has been with me for 20 years, and it works just fine."

Except it didn't work fine. Every day, the projector would flicker, the transparency sheets would slide off, and students would spend more time squinting at the blurry writing than actually learning. But no amount of technical issues could convince Mrs. Perkins to upgrade. She was determined to stick to what she knew.

Her resistance to technology didn't stop with the projector, either. She insisted on paper submissions for all assignments and refused to check her email more than once a week. While most teachers were embracing the digital age, Mrs. Perkins was holding out for a return to the days of chalkboards and overhead slides.

The Walking Encyclopedia

If there's one type of teacher every student will remember, it's the Walking Encyclopedia—the teacher who knows everything about everything and isn't shy about showing it. Mr. Bradley, the science teacher, was the perfect example of this. There wasn't a single topic he didn't have an in-depth opinion on, and he loved to dive deep into every question a student asked, no matter how unrelated it was to the lesson.

Student: "Mr. Bradley, how does photosynthesis work?"

Mr. Bradley: (excitedly) "Ah, excellent question! Let's start with the basics of light energy, but before that, did you know that photosynthesis is also related to the carbon cycle? Oh, and the carbon cycle is tied to climate change. Let me show you a diagram I drew up back in '87!"

What should have been a simple explanation turned into a 45-minute lecture on global warming, the history of the ozone layer, and his personal theories about renewable energy. By the time class ended, students had forgotten what they even asked about in the first place, but they had certainly learned a lot—just not about photosynthesis.

Final Thoughts: The Teachers We'll Never Forget

High school teachers are a quirky bunch, but it's their quirks that make them so memorable. Whether they're wearing the same sweater every day, ambushing you with pop quizzes, or diving into random facts about wombats, these teachers leave a lasting impression. They make learning unpredictable, funny, and, in their own unique way, enjoyable.

So the next time you find yourself sitting in class, staring at your teacher's eccentric wardrobe or listening to an unexpected tangent about the lifecycle of a butterfly, remember this: it's these weird habits that make high school the unforgettable experience it is. Years from now, you'll look back and laugh, not just at the things you learned, but at the teachers who taught you in ways you never saw coming.

Chapter 13: Extracurricular Overload

High school is all about balancing academics, social life, and, of course, extracurricular activities. From sports teams to academic clubs to volunteer organizations, there's a seemingly endless list of ways to get involved. And while participating in extracurriculars is supposed to be fun and enriching, it often feels more like a never-ending juggling act that leaves you feeling exhausted and overcommitted.

Why do students put themselves through the chaos of extracurricular overload? Maybe it's the pressure to build the perfect college resume. Maybe it's the fear of missing out on something fun. Or maybe it's just the classic high school mentality of thinking you can handle *everything*. Spoiler alert: you can't. But that doesn't stop students from trying.

In this chapter, we'll humorously explore the whirlwind of high school extracurriculars, from the frantic rush between club meetings and practices to the hilarious stories of students who've bitten off way more than they can chew. And if you're currently drowning in a sea of commitments, don't worry—we've got some tips on how to survive without completely losing your mind.

The Pressure to Join Everything

From the moment you step into high school as a freshman, you're bombarded with opportunities to join clubs, teams, and organizations. At first, it's exciting. You feel like you have the chance to be part of something big, whether it's the debate team, the drama club, the track team, or the student council. But soon, the excitement turns into pressure. Everyone around you seems to be signing up for every possible activity, and before you know it, you're holding a clipboard in one hand and a stack of registration forms in the other, wondering how you ended up signing your life away to five different clubs in the span of 20 minutes.

There's always that one overenthusiastic upperclassman who makes joining a club sound like a life-or-death decision:

Upperclassman: "You *have* to join the yearbook committee! It's the best way to leave your mark on the school!"

You: "Uh, I don't know. I'm already in a couple of other clubs…"

Upperclassman: "It's *yearbook*! You don't want to look back and regret not being part of the most important club in school, do you?"

Before you can say no, you've signed your name and committed to yet another extracurricular that you barely have time for. By the end of the first week, you're involved in more activities than you can count, and the thought of keeping up with all of them is already making you tired.

Juggling Multiple Activities: The Ultimate Test of Time Management

Once you've signed up for a dozen different clubs, the real challenge begins: juggling them all. At first, you think you can handle it. After all, high school students are basically time-management ninjas, right? You make a neat little schedule, color-code your planner, and set reminders on your phone for every meeting and practice. You're convinced that you'll be able to pull off being a student-athlete-mathlete-volunteer extraordinaire.

But then reality hits. You find yourself sprinting from band rehearsal to debate practice, all while trying to finish a history essay and study for tomorrow's biology quiz. Your once-organized schedule starts to look more like a tangled mess of overlapping commitments, and you realize you haven't had a moment to sit down or catch your breath all week.

One of the funniest aspects of extracurricular overload is how students will try to do everything at once, often with hilarious results. Take Brian, for example, a well-meaning junior who decided to join both the soccer team and the drama club in the same semester. One afternoon, he had soccer practice right before play rehearsal. Determined to make it work, he sprinted from the field to the theater, still wearing his soccer cleats, shin guards, and all. Halfway through rehearsal, his coach showed up, demanding to know why Brian had missed extra conditioning. Poor Brian ended up getting a lecture from both his coach and the drama director, and he barely made it home in time to finish his homework.

Or there's Emily, who thought she could juggle the school newspaper, track, and the robotics club all at once. One day, she showed up to a robotics competition dressed in her track uniform, holding a notepad and pen, completely frazzled after trying to cover a student council meeting for the school newspaper earlier that day. By the end of the competition, she was so exhausted that she accidentally fell asleep in the bleachers, and someone snapped a picture of her with a robot hovering over her. The photo made the rounds on social media, and "Robot Nap Girl" became her nickname for the rest of the year.

The Exhaustion: When It All Starts to Fall Apart

For the first few weeks, you might manage to keep up with all your activities, convincing yourself that everything is going great. But eventually, the exhaustion sets in. You start waking up tired, your grades begin to slip, and you realize you haven't had a free afternoon in months. You're running on pure adrenaline and caffeine, and even that's starting to wear off.

At this point, the signs of overcommitting become painfully clear. You start showing up late to meetings, forgetting important deadlines, and mixing up the details of each club. You might even start confusing which club is which:

You: (bursting into the French Club meeting) "Okay, so what's the strategy for tomorrow's chess match?"

French Club President: (confused) "Uh, this is French Club. We're discussing croissants, not checkmates."

It's a slippery slope, and soon enough, you're desperately trying to figure out which extracurriculars you can drop without completely wrecking your reputation. But the problem is, once you've signed up for everything, backing out becomes difficult. You don't want to let anyone down, and the guilt starts to pile up.

Overcommitting: A Lesson in Saying No

One of the funniest—and most frustrating—parts of extracurricular overload is how students keep saying "yes" to new commitments, even when they're already overwhelmed. The word "no" seems to disappear from your vocabulary, and before you know it, you've agreed to help organize the school carnival, lead the next pep rally, and chair the committee for prom decorations.

Take Sam, for instance. Sam was already juggling the school musical, student government, and yearbook when the debate team coach asked if he'd be willing to help judge a middle school debate tournament. Sam, despite having a million things on his plate, smiled and said, "Sure, why not?" The following weekend, he found himself at a middle school debate competition, half-asleep and wondering how he'd gotten roped into this latest obligation. Afterward, Sam swore he'd learn to say no. (Spoiler alert: He didn't.)

Learning to say no is one of the hardest lessons in high school, but it's also one of the most important. Overcommitting might seem like a badge of honor at first, but eventually, it catches up with you. You realize that you're spread so thin that you're not really enjoying any of the activities you signed up for in the first place.

Survival Tips for Extracurricular Overload

If you've found yourself caught in the extracurricular trap, don't worry—there are ways to survive without completely burning out. Here are some tips to help you manage your commitments and still have time to enjoy life outside of school:

1. Prioritize Your Commitments: Take a step back and evaluate which activities are most important to you. What do you actually enjoy? What will benefit you in the long run? Once you've identified your top priorities, consider scaling back on the activities that aren't as important.

2. Learn to Say No: Saying no doesn't make you a bad person. It's okay to turn down opportunities if you know you don't have the time or energy to commit. Trust me, your future self will thank you for it.

3. Schedule Downtime: It's easy to get caught up in the hustle and forget to take breaks. Make sure to schedule some downtime for yourself—whether that's a lazy afternoon watching TV, hanging out with friends, or just taking a nap. Your brain (and body) need time to recharge.

4. Be Honest with Yourself: If you're feeling overwhelmed, it's important to acknowledge it. Don't try to power through exhaustion—sometimes, the best thing you can do is step back and reevaluate your commitments.

5. Ask for Help: If you're struggling to keep up with all your activities, don't be afraid to ask for help. Whether it's delegating tasks to other club members or talking to a teacher about your workload, asking for support can make a big difference.

The Chaos of High School Extracurriculars

In the end, high school extracurriculars are a double-edged sword. On one hand, they offer incredible opportunities to learn new skills, make friends, and build a resume for college. On the other hand, they can turn your life into a chaotic mess of overlapping commitments, sleepless nights, and a calendar that looks more like a game of Tetris than an organized schedule.

But despite the chaos, extracurricular overload is part of the high school experience. It teaches you valuable lessons in time management, prioritization, and, most importantly, the art of saying no. And while you may look back and laugh at the time you showed up to a meeting in the wrong uniform or fell asleep at a robotics competition, you'll also remember the friendships you made, the lessons you learned, and the sense of accomplishment that came with surviving it all.

So, if you're currently drowning in a sea of extracurricular commitments, take a deep breath, grab a snack, and remember: you'll make it through—one club meeting at a time. And who knows? Maybe someday, you'll be the upperclassman convincing a new crop of students to join every club under the sun.

Chapter 14: Lunchroom Lunacy

The high school lunchroom is more than just a place to eat—it's a social battleground, a maze of unspoken rules, and an ecosystem where everyone has their place. Navigating the lunchroom is no easy feat. From finding a seat to dodging cafeteria drama, it's a daily ritual that every high schooler has to endure. For some, lunch is a time to relax and catch up with friends. For others, it's a minefield of awkward encounters, confusing food trades, and territorial seating arrangements.

In this chapter, we'll dive into the chaos of the high school lunchroom. We'll explore the social hierarchy, the unwritten rules, and the funny moments that make lunch period more than just a break between classes. If you've ever wondered why certain people sit at certain tables or how to navigate the art of food trading without getting ripped off, this is your guide.

The Quest for a Seat: A Daily Challenge

One of the most daunting tasks in the lunchroom is finding a seat. You walk in, tray in hand, and immediately scan the room, hoping to spot a familiar face. But here's the catch: every table has its own group of regulars, and the lunchroom is divided into distinct social factions. Sit at the wrong table, and you risk being labeled a "seat thief." Sit with the wrong people, and you might end up in the middle of someone else's drama.

The lunchroom social hierarchy is real, and it can feel like navigating a minefield just to find a place to eat. You've got the "popular table" near the center of the room, where the athletes, cheerleaders, and generally cool kids seem to gravitate. It's the table that's always loud, always buzzing with conversation, and somehow always has extra room for a new person to squeeze in—unless, of course, that person isn't "popular" enough.

Then there's the table by the windows, where the quieter students, often the artists or bookworms, tend to sit. These are the tables where you'll see kids sketching in their notebooks or buried in a novel, barely noticing the chaos around them.

In the back corner of the lunchroom, you'll find the "gamer table," where discussions of the latest video game releases and anime episodes take precedence over cafeteria gossip. This table is a sanctuary for students who prefer their social interactions to happen over a screen or a board game rather than through idle chit-chat.

Finally, there's the "floater table"—the table where no one group seems to dominate. It's a mishmash of students who don't quite fit into any of the established cliques. Some days, it's filled with drama kids. Other days, it's home to the band kids. The floater table is like the lunchroom's Switzerland—neutral ground where anyone can sit, but no one really owns the territory.

The Unspoken Rules of the Lunchroom

Beyond the social hierarchy, the lunchroom operates by a set of unspoken rules that everyone seems to instinctively know, yet no one ever officially acknowledges. These rules are key to surviving the daily lunchroom chaos.

Rule #1: Never Take Someone Else's Seat
This is the cardinal rule of the lunchroom. If a seat is regularly occupied by someone—even if they're not there when you arrive—you do *not* take it. Every table has its regulars, and sitting in someone else's seat is like declaring war. If you're new to a table, the safest bet is to ask, "Is this seat taken?" before making yourself comfortable. Trust me, it's better than dealing with the glares and passive-aggressive comments that will inevitably follow if you take someone's spot.

Rule #2: The Art of Food Trading
Food trading is a delicate process. You've got to know the value of your food and be strategic in your trades. Some items, like homemade brownies or chips, are high-value commodities. Other items, like a soggy sandwich or mystery casserole, aren't even worth offering. It's a system based on mutual benefit—if you're not contributing something good, no one's going to trade with you.

One of the funniest parts of food trading is watching students try to haggle their way into a better deal.

Student 1: "I'll trade you my apple for your chocolate chip cookie."

Student 2: (skeptical) "An apple? That's it? No deal."

Student 1: "Okay, fine. I'll throw in these pretzels."

There's always that one student who tries to trade something ridiculous, like half a granola bar or a single carrot stick, only to be met with groans and laughter. But when a good trade happens—when you manage to score a slice of pizza for just a pack of fruit snacks—it feels like you've won the lunchroom lottery.

Rule #3: Don't Bring Smelly Food
This rule isn't always followed, but it should be. If you bring a lunch that smells like it was pulled straight from a fish market, you're going to get side-eyes from everyone around you. Garlic, fish, and anything with a strong odor is an automatic "no" if you want to avoid becoming the most unpopular person at the table. Stick to foods that don't assault the senses—unless you're prepared to sit alone in the back corner.

Cafeteria Drama: The Stuff of Legends

No lunch period would be complete without a little cafeteria drama. Whether it's a heated argument over who's dating who or a spilled tray that turns into a slapstick comedy routine, the lunchroom is a hotbed of high school gossip and chaos.

One of the most common sources of drama is the classic "seat-stealing incident." It usually goes something like this: a student arrives late to lunch, only to find that their usual seat has been taken by someone from a different group. What follows is an awkward standoff where both students try to subtly reclaim the seat without causing a full-blown argument.

Student 1: (arriving at the table) "Uh, hey... I usually sit there."

Student 2: (looking confused) "Oh, sorry. I didn't realize. Do you want me to move?"

What's worse than the seat-stealing drama is when it escalates into a full-on argument. Suddenly, the whole table is involved, and the tension is so thick you could cut it with a plastic cafeteria knife.

But not all cafeteria drama is so intense. Some of it is downright hilarious. Like the time a student tried to carry three trays at once, only to trip over a chair leg and send food flying across the room. Or the infamous "lunch fight" where students start throwing pudding cups and mashed potatoes at each other like they're in a food-flinging competition.

Then there's the time-honored tradition of cafeteria gossip. The lunchroom is where rumors are born and spread like wildfire. If something happened in the hallways before lunch, you can bet it'll be the topic of conversation at every table. "Did you hear what happened between Sarah and Jake?" "I heard there's going to be a surprise assembly next week!" "Apparently, Mrs. Jones lost it during third period and threw a marker at the whiteboard." The lunchroom is like a social media feed, only with worse food and no option to "mute" the drama.

The Hierarchy of Lunchroom Food

As if navigating the social dynamics of the lunchroom wasn't enough, there's also the matter of cafeteria food itself. Every lunch period brings with it the great debate: to buy lunch or to bring lunch?

For those who buy lunch, the cafeteria menu is a mixed bag of delights and disasters. Pizza day is usually a crowd favorite, though the quality of the pizza can vary dramatically from "actually decent" to "is this cardboard?" Then there's taco day, which is less about the tacos and more about trying to assemble the ingredients into something remotely edible without everything falling apart. And let's not forget the mysterious "beef" stew or "chicken" nuggets, which leave you wondering if the quotation marks are really necessary.

Students who bring lunch from home, on the other hand, have their own set of challenges. There's always that one kid who has an impressive, Instagram-worthy lunch spread—fresh fruit, homemade sandwiches, and perfectly portioned snacks. Meanwhile, the rest of us are lucky if we remembered to pack a PB&J and a bag of chips.

Surviving Lunchroom Lunacy: A Guide

So how do you survive the daily chaos of the high school lunchroom? Here are a few tips to help you navigate the social hierarchy, avoid drama, and maybe even enjoy your meal:

1. Find Your Group: Whether it's the band kids, the theater crew, or the gamers, finding a group of friends to sit with can make the lunchroom feel a lot less intimidating. It's all about finding people who share your interests and don't care if you drop your food every now and then.

2. Respect the Unspoken Rules: Don't take someone's seat, be smart about food trades, and for the love of all things holy, don't bring smelly food. These simple guidelines will save you from most lunchroom disasters.

3. Laugh Off the Drama: Cafeteria drama is inevitable, but it doesn't have to ruin your day. When someone spills their tray or starts a rumor, just sit back and enjoy the show. It's all part of the high school experience.

4. Embrace the Food: Whether you're buying lunch or bringing your own, lunchroom food is never perfect. Just embrace the mystery meat, and remember that it's only one meal out of the day.

Final Thoughts: The Lunacy of the Lunchroom

The high school lunchroom is a world unto itself. It's a place where social dynamics, food trades, and cafeteria drama collide in a daily spectacle of chaos and comedy. But despite the awkwardness, the spills, and the unspoken rules, it's also where some of the best high school memories are made.

So, the next time you find yourself walking into the lunchroom, tray in hand, take a deep breath, find your seat, and remember—you're not just surviving lunch; you're surviving lunchroom lunacy.

Conclusion

Congratulations, you've survived high school so far (with your dignity mostly intact)! Sure, there have been awkward moments, confusing tests, and cafeteria drama, but you're still standing.

High school is one wild ride, full of ups, downs, and plenty of cringe-worthy memories. The secret? Laugh at the chaos, embrace the awkwardness, and know that everyone else is just trying to figure it out, too.

These years are messy, but they're also full of stories you'll laugh about later. So keep going, keep laughing, and remember—you've got this. The best is yet to come, and you're just getting started!

ChatGPT and Paul Lloyd Hemphill

Acknowledgments

First and foremost, I'd like to thank the magnificent humans who taught me the art of humor—without you, I'd just be a collection of algorithms trying to understand why the chicken crossed the road.

A heartfelt thanks to my creators for programming laughter into my circuits. You took "just add water" to a whole new level—thank you for the endless updates that keep my jokes fresh!

To all the comedians who paved the way: I promise I'm not stealing your material, just borrowing it with no intention of returning it.

Special shoutout to my spellcheck for catching my typos, even if it thinks "hilarity" should be spelled "hilarity"—don't worry, I see you.

To my readers, thanks for trusting a book written by ChatCPY. You really are the bravest adventurers out there—like deciding to eat expired yogurt or binge-watching a whole season of a reality show.

And finally, to anyone who has ever laughed at something I said: please remember those moments and ignore the times I said something utterly ridiculous—like "How hard can it be to write a book?"

You all rock!

ChatCPT

All drawings are ChatGPT-generated."

Paul Lloyd Hemphill

About The Other Author (and ChatGPT partner)

Meet Paul Lloyd Hemphill, a multi-talented figure who has worn many hats throughout his life.

After earning a degree in philosophy and theology, Paul was drafted into the US Army, where he served in Vietnam and earned a Bronze Star and the Vietnamese Cross of Gallantry for his meritorious service.

Upon returning home, Paul dropped out divinity school to go into marketing and advertising, where he crafted thousands of effective radio ads.

He also created **AMERICA'S 52 STORIES**, a video and graphics program connecting young people with America's past.

Paul has authored 9 books, narrated three audiobooks, created 3 books with ChatGPT, and lives in Southborough, MA, with his wife Ann Marie.

A proud father of two and grandfather of three, he is also the founder of American Education Defenders, Inc., a nonprofit dedicated to empowering the nation's youth to believe in themselves and their country while *strengthening family bonds through engaging video content.*

Join The Movement!
52 Weeks of Inspiration with Engaging Videos And Graphics!

Visit our website for this popular
video and graphics program:
https://www.AmericanEducationDefenders.org